Vegetarian
Cuisine

Dedicated to my husband, Cecil

Dr. Betty "K"
author of the best-selling *Caribbean Cuisine*

Delicious International Flavours
Simple, Easy-to-Prepare Recipes

Front Cover:
Vegetarian Stir-Fry, page 72
Peppery Rice Salad, page 58
Sada Roti, page 96

Vegetarian Cuisine
by
Dr. Betty "K"

Fourth Printing — November 2002

Copyright © 1993 by
Betty K Books & Food
3 — 1750 The Queensway
Suite 1305
Etobicoke, Ontario
M9C 5H5

Canadian Cataloguing in Publication Data

K., Betty, —

Vegetarian cuisine

ISBN 1-895292-18-2

1. Vegetarian cookery.   I. Title.

TX837.K2 1993   641.5'636   C93-098041-7

Raku plates and bowls created by potter Donovan Chester
Courtesy of Collections Fine Art Gallery
Regina, Saskatchewan

Glasses by glass artist Robert Held
Vancouver, B.C.

Photography by:
Patricia Holdsworth
Patricia Holdsworth Photography
Regina, Saskatchewan

Designed, Printed and Produced in Canada by:
Centax Books, a Division of PrintWest Communications Ltd.
Publishing Director, Photo Designer & Food Stylist: Margo Embury
1150 Eighth Avenue, Regina, Saskatchewan, Canada S4R 1C9
(306) 525-2304   FAX (306) 757-2439

Table of Contents

Nutritional Analysis Key — In the following recipes:

light butter is 39% m.f.
low-fat Cheddar is 7% m.f.
low-fat mozzarella is 15% m.f.
low-fat yogurt is 0.1% m.f.
skim milk feta cheese is 15% m.f.
light sour cream is 6.7% m.f.

Nutritional analysis does not include optional ingredients.

Soya mince and soya cubes are dehydrated soya protein products. They are available under several brand names in health food stores.

Recipes have been tested in U.S. Standard measurements. Common metric measurements are given as a convenience for those who are more familiar with metric. Recipes have not been tested in metric.

Introduction

I was born in Georgetown, Guyana, a former British Colony located on the northern coast of South America. I pursued undergraduate studies at McGill University, Montreal, then went on to study Medicine at the Royal College of Surgeons in Dublin, Ireland. I have lived and practiced in Ireland, England, Trinidad, Guyana and Canada.

The inspiration for writing *Vegetarian Cuisine* came from my friends and from my cousin in Barbados, Mr. Latchman Kissoon. He suggested that I write a vegetarian cookbook and add the nutritional analysis so that vegetarians would know the protein, carbohydrate and fat value of the recipes.

This book is not a diet book. It is simply a vegetarian cookbook with an international flavour, written in a simple format with easy-to-prepare recipes.

The ingredients are readily available in large supermarkets, Oriental and West Indian grocery stores. I hope both vegetarians and nonvegetarians will enjoy this book.

Acknowledgements

I would like to thank my relatives and friends who have given me suggestions and recipes for this book.

My thanks to my mother-in-law, Mrs. S.N. Singh, and my mother, Mrs. R. Kissoon, for their contribution of recipes. I would also like to thank my dear friend, Mrs. Ruth Thomson, for the recipe for her special Carrot Cake.

I would like to thank my friend, Margo Embury, for all her help, her suggestions and patience in putting this book together.

Thank you to my daughter, Nadia Singh, for typing my manuscript.

And, a special thank you to my husband, Cecil, for his encouragement and hard work in marketing *Caribbean Cuisine*, and for his enthusiasm and support for this new book, *Vegetarian Cuisine*.

Eating Vegetarian Style

The vegetarian diet has been embraced by the majority of mankind throughout history. Millions of people in India, China and Japan have been vegetarians for thousands of years. In the west, the ancient Greeks promoted a vegetarian diet. From Plato and Plutarch to Isaac Newton, Benjamin Franklin, Albert Einstein, Leonardo da Vinci, Leo Tolstoy, Albert Schweitzer, George Bernard Shaw, Martin Luther and John Wesley, numerous scientists and philosophers have advocated a vegetarian diet.

At a time when meat is more readily accessible to more people than ever before, vegetarianism is attracting millions of new recruits. Today, around the world, meat and fish supply only 11 percent of the food energy consumed from all sources. Health concerns, economic reasons, religious, environmental and philosophical beliefs are all important in this increased interest in eating vegetarian style. There are several types of vegetarians. **Vegans** do not eat any foods of animal origin, including dairy products, eggs and sometimes even honey. **Lacto-vegetarians** consume dairy products. **Lacto-ovo-vegetarians** consume both dairy products and eggs. **Semi-vegetarians** are a rapidly growing new group who consume small amounts of meat and fish while consuming mostly whole grains, vegetables, fruit and dairy products.

Studies of vegetarian groups have shown a lower incidence of heart disease, stroke, diabetes, colon and other cancers, osteoporosis and obesity than in nonvegetarian groups. The vegetarian diet does require some thought and planning to ensure a well-balanced diet. Plant proteins are incomplete so it is important to combine protein sources that complement one another. Eat grains (rice, corn, nuts, seeds or whole-grain breads) with legumes (beans, lentils or split peas). Eat peanut butter with whole-grain bread or combine whole-wheat flour with soya flour. Soya beans and soya bean products are the most complete of the plant foods. Most vegetarian sources used to say that these combinations must be eaten at each meal. New studies show that the body stores amino acids and combines them over a period of time to fulfill its protein requirements. Although exact food combinations are not required in the same meal, they should be eaten over the course of a day; it is desirable to have all of the amino acids present in the digestive system. It is important to choose a wide variety of cereals, whole-grain breads, legumes, nuts, seeds, fruits and vegetables. Including dairy products and eggs in the vegetarian diet makes it relatively easy to obtain adequate nutrients. Children and pregnant women have greater nutritional needs and they should receive special consideration. There are many excellent nutritional books that give specific information for eating vegetarian style.

Over the centuries, many diverse cultures have specialized in vegetarian cuisines. They have developed delicious and innovative flavour combinations. Many of the most authentic and tantalizing ethnic dishes are vegetarian in nature. Originally the word vegetarian was derived from the Latin *vegetare* which means to enliven and *vegetus* which means active or vigorous. With the current trend towards fitness, good health and increased physical activity, millions of North Americans are eating vegetarian style. They are seeking out recipes from other cultures and cuisines where there is a respected tradition of vegetarian cooking. Restaurants are finding less demand for meat dishes and more interest in salads, fresh fruit and fruit juices.

For vegetarians, semi-vegetarians and those who just want delicious, healthy recipes to add to their daily menus, *Vegetarian Cuisine* is a treasure. These recipes come from Doctor Betty "K"'s Caribbean heritage which has been enriched by the cuisines of India, Africa, Asia, Europe, North and South America. Flavours and aromas range from subtle to fiery, from rich and full-bodied to light and refreshing.

Whether good health or great flavour is your goal, you will enjoy both in *Vegetarian Cuisine*.

Appetizers
&
Drinks

Avocado Dip

Pepper sauce gives this velvety dip added tang.

2	medium avocados	2
2	garlic cloves, minced	2
1 tsp.	lemon juice	5 mL
1 tsp.	hot pepper sauce	5 mL
	salt and pepper to taste	
8 oz.	light cream cheese, softened*	250 g

1. Peel avocados. Mash with a fork.
2. Mix in minced garlic, lemon juice, pepper sauce, salt and pepper.
3. Beat cream cheese until light and blend into avocado mixture.

Serve with vegetables, crackers or corn chips.

Yields 2 cups (500 mL)

*8 oz. (250 g) soft tofu could be substituted for cream cheese.

See photograph on page 17.

2 cups (500 mL)

Energy	— Calories	1263	Cholesterol	115 mg
	— kJ	5286	Carbohydrate	47 g
Protein		34 g	Sodium	2268 mg
Total Fat		112 g		

Cucumber Dip

A light refreshing dip with the zesty flavour of chili powder.

1/2 cup	natural yogurt	125 mL
4 oz.	light cream cheese	125 mL
1 tsp.	grated onion	5 mL
1 tsp.	chili powder	5 mL
	salt and pepper to taste	
1	medium cucumber, peeled, finely chopped or grated	1

Cucumber Dip

(Continued)

1. Blend yogurt, cream cheese, onion, chili powder, salt and pepper.
2. Fold in cucumber. Chill. Serve with vegetables or crackers.

Yields 1 cup (250 mL)

See photograph on page 17.

1 cup (250 mL)

Energy — Calories	291	Cholesterol	58 mg
— kJ	1216	Carbohydrate	13 g
Protein	16 g	Sodium	1153 mg
Total Fat	19 g		

Eggplant and Tomato Dip

1	eggplant	1
1	garlic clove	1
1	tomato	1
1	small onion, finely chopped	1
	salt and pepper to taste	
1 tsp.	hot pepper sauce	5 mL

1. Make a slit about 1" (2.5 cm) in length on each side of eggplant.
2. Halve garlic clove and place 1 half in each slit.
3. Grill eggplant until tender and pulp is soft, about 20-30 minutes.
4. Remove from heat, peel off skin. Mash eggplant pulp and garlic.
5. Grill tomato until soft, 5-10 minutes. Peel tomato, chop tomato finely and add to eggplant mixture with onion, salt, pepper and pepper sauce. Stir well. Serve with pita pockets or crackers.

Yields 1 cup (250 mL)

See photograph on page 17.

1 cup (250 mL)

Energy — Calories	84	Cholesterol	0 mg
— kJ	349	Carbohydrate	19 g
Protein	4 g	Sodium	37 mg
Total Fat	.6 g		

Savoury Cheesecake

Serve this appetizer with green grapes or with a green salad and whole-wheat rolls for a light lunch.

1 cup	graham wafer crumbs	250 mL
¼ cup	butter, melted	60 mL
½ cup	1% evaporated milk	125 mL
1	lemon, juice and rind of	1
8 oz.	light cream cheese	250 g
2	celery stalks, finely chopped	2
2 tbsp.	sultana raisins	30 mL
2 tbsp.	walnuts	30 mL
1	apple, coarsely chopped	1
¼ tsp.	grated nutmeg	1 mL
	olives and paprika to garnish	

1. Combine graham crumbs with melted butter. Press over sides and base of 8" (20 cm) pie plate. Refrigerate for 1-2 hours.
2. Combine evaporated milk with grated rind and juice of a lemon. Whip until thick, add cream cheese and continue to beat.
3. Stir celery, raisins, walnuts, apple and nutmeg into cheese mixture.
4. Pour filling into pie shell. Garnish with olives and paprika. Refrigerate for 4-6 hours. Serve on plates in small wedges.

Serves 6

1 Serving

Energy	**— Calories**	352	**Cholesterol**	53 mg
	— kJ	1472	**Carbohydrate**	31 g
Protein		9 g	**Sodium**	706 mg
Total Fat		23 g		

Apples have been cultivated for over 3,000 years and there are thousands of varieties. They are a good source of vitamins A and C and are helpful in elimination.

Eggplant Fritters

In Guyana these East Indian fritters are also known as "Bigani."

1	eggplant, thinly sliced	1
	salt and pepper to taste	
½ tsp.	garlic powder	2 mL
½ tsp.	chili powder	2 mL
¼ cup	flour	60 mL
	vegetable oil for frying	

BATTER:

½ cup	ground dried split peas	125 mL
½ tsp.	garlic powder	2 mL
½ tsp.	hot pepper sauce	2 mL
	salt and pepper to taste	
	water	

1. Sprinkle sliced eggplant with salt, pepper, garlic powder and chili powder. Let stand 20-30 minutes.
2. Combine all batter ingredients. Add enough water to make batter the consistency of thick cream.
3. Toss each piece of eggplant in flour, shake off excess flour, then dip into prepared batter.
4. Heat oil to 365°F (185°C). Deep-fry eggplant in hot oil. Drain on paper towels. Serve warm.

Makes about 24 slices

1 Slice (oil for frying not included)

Energy	— Calories	28	**Cholesterol**	0 mg
	— kJ	119	**Carbohydrate**	5 g
Protein		2 g	**Sodium**	3 mg
Total Fat		.08 g		

Eggplant is low in calories and it helps balance diets that are high in protein and starch.

Pumpkin Fritters

The rich pumpkin flavour makes these crunchy fritters a special treat.

1 lb.	pumpkin, peeled and diced	500 g
2 tbsp.	sugar	30 mL
1 tbsp.	light butter	15 mL
2	eggs, lightly beaten	2
⅓ cup	flour	75 mL
½ cup	vegetable oil for frying	125 mL

1. Boil diced pumpkin until tender, approximately 30 minutes.
2. Drain. Mash cooked pumpkin, add sugar, butter and eggs, stirring well. Add flour slowly and keep stirring.
3. Drop 1 tbsp. (15 mL) of batter into hot oil in a frying pan and fry to a golden brown. Drain on paper towels. Serve warm.

Makes about 20

1 Fritter (oil for frying not included)

Energy	— Calories	28	Cholesterol	23 mg
	— kJ	116	Carbohydrate	4 g
Protein		0.9 g	Sodium	10 mg
Total Fat		0.8 g		

Native to the Americas, pumpkin is high in potassium, low in carbohydrates. It is a good source of vitamin A and a fair source of vitamins B and C.

Spinach Cakes

These nutritious patties are full of flavour.

8 oz.	spinach leaves	250 g
2	eggs, lightly beaten	2
1	small onion, chopped	1
2 tbsp.	light margarine or butter	30 mL
1/2 cup	flour	125 mL
1/2 tsp.	baking powder	2 mL
1/2 cup	bread crumbs	125 mL
	salt and pepper to taste	
1/2 cup	milk	125 mL
1/2 cup	vegetable oil for frying	125 mL

1. Wash spinach leaves. Steam until wilted; run under cold water. Squeeze out excess water, pat dry in paper towels. Chop finely.
2. Combine spinach, eggs, onion and butter.
3. Add flour, baking powder, breadcrumbs, salt and pepper. Blend well.
4. Add enough milk to spinach mixture to make a thick batter.
5. Scoop out batter with a tablespoon, drop into hot oil in a frying pan and fry until golden brown. Drain on paper towels.

Makes 12-15

1 Cake (if making 12)   (oil for frying not included)

Energy	— Calories	80	Cholesterol	46 mg
	— kJ	335	Carbohydrate	9 g
Protein		3 g	Sodium	114 mg
Total Fat		3 g		

Spinach is a very good source of vitamins A and C plus iron and potassium.

Split Pea Ball

"Phulourie" is an East Indian vegetarian specialty.

1 cup	ground dried split peas	250 mL
1/4 cup	flour	60 mL
	water	
1	small onion, finely chopped	1
2	garlic cloves, minced	2
1/2 tsp.	cumin powder	2 mL
	salt and pepper to taste	
1/2 tsp.	curry powder	2 mL
1/2 tsp.	hot pepper sauce	2 mL
	vegetable oil for frying	

1. Mix ground peas and flour with enough water to make a thick batter.
2. Add all remaining ingredients and beat well, until light and fluffy.
3. Form the pea mixture into small balls and fry in hot oil (365°F [185°]) until golden brown. Drain on paper towels. Serve warm.

Makes 24

1 Serving (1 ball) (oil for frying not included)

Energy	— Calories	49	Cholesterol	0 mg
	— kJ	209	Carbohydrate	9 g
Protein		3 g	Sodium	5 mg
Total Fat		0.1 g		

Split peas, like beans, are high in protein and low in carbohydrates and fat.

Vegetarian Fish Fingers

This tasty appetizer has similarities to the Italian Polenta and the Southern Hush Puppies which are made from cornmeal. Serve as an appetizer or with your favourite salad for lunch.

1 cup	1% milk	250 mL
½ cup	Cream of Wheat	125 mL
¾ cup	grated Cheddar cheese	175 mL
	salt and pepper to taste	
½ tsp.	Betty K seasoning or	2 mL
	seasoned salt	
½ cup	bread crumbs	125 mL
	vegetable oil for frying	

1. Bring milk to a boil, add Cream of Wheat, cheese, salt, pepper and Betty K seasoning. Mix quickly and cook for a few minutes, until thick and smooth.
2. Spread Cream of Wheat mixture on a flat board; cut into strips ¾ x 2" (2 x 5 cm).
3. Roll strips in bread crumbs. Heat oil in frying pan and fry fingers until golden brown, about 5 minutes. Drain on paper towels. Serve warm.

Makes about 20 fingers

1 Finger (oil for frying not included)

Energy	— Calories	37	Cholesterol	2 mg
	— kJ	158	Carbohydrate	6 g
Protein		2 g	Sodium	108 mg
Total Fat		0.6 g		

Cream of Wheat or farina contains the wheat germ but not the wheat bran. It is prepared from the hulled wheat kernel.

Italian "Meatballs"

These mock "meatballs" have a delicious garlic and oregano-flavoured tomato sauce.

2 cups	Betty K soya mince	500 mL
½ cup	water	125 mL
1 tbsp.	minced onion	15 mL
1 tsp.	crushed garlic	5 mL
	salt and pepper to taste	
1 tsp.	oregano	5 mL
1	egg, beaten	1
3 tbsp.	vegetable oil	45 mL
2 cups	tomato juice	500 mL

1. Mix together soya mince, water, onion, garlic, salt, pepper and oregano.
2. Add beaten egg and mix well. Form soya mixture into walnut-sized balls.
3. Heat oil and brown balls on all sides. Drain off any leftover oil. Add tomato juice, cover and simmer for 10-15 minutes, until soya softens.

Makes 24 meatballs

1 Meatball (oil for frying not included)

Energy — Calories	32	Cholesterol	11 mg
— kJ	135	Carbohydrate	3 g
Protein	3 g	Sodium	30 mg
Total Fat	1 g		

Note: *Soya Mince is a textured dehydrated soya protein made from soya flour. It is available under several brand names in health food stores.*

Soya beans are rich in proteins; they contain all eight amino acids and are also rich in most minerals and vitamins.

Appetizers — from lower left

Eggplant and Tomato Dip, page 9
Avocado Dip, page 8
Carrot Drink, page 22
Cucumber Dip, page 8
Pita Bread, page 98

Stuffed Mushrooms

These baked mushrooms have a tangy fresh tomato filling.

12	large mushrooms	12
3 tbsp.	olive oil	75 mL
2	large tomatoes, peeled and finely chopped	2
1	garlic clove, minced	1
2 tsp.	dried chives	10 mL
1 tbsp.	grated onion	15 mL
	salt and pepper to taste	
1/2 tsp.	hot pepper sauce (optional)	2 mL
1/2 tbsp.	lemon juice	7.5 mL

1. Wash mushrooms and wipe clean. Remove stems.
2. Lightly oil a baking sheet and place mushrooms on it. Pour 1/2 tsp. (2 mL) olive oil over each mushroom, bake at 350°F (180°C) for 20 minutes. Cool.
3. Combine tomatoes, garlic, chives, onion, salt, pepper, hot pepper sauce and lemon juice with remaining olive oil.
4. Fill each mushroom cap with mixture.

Makes 12 mushroom caps

1 Mushroom Cap

Energy — Calories	42	Cholesterol	0 mg
— kJ	175	Carbohydrate	2 g
Protein	0.7 g	Sodium	3 mg
Total Fat	4 g		

Mushrooms were prized in ancient Egypt, the Pharaohs restricted them to their own tables. The Romans served them at festivals and thought that they gave strength to their warriors. Mushrooms are low in calories and are a good source of vitamin B.

Cheese Rolls

These rolls will please both cheese-lovers and vegetarians.

PASTRY:

1¹/₂ cups	flour	375 mL
1 tsp.	salt	5 mL
¹/₂ cup	low-fat margarine	125 mL
¹/₂ cup	ice-water	125 mL

FILLING:

³/₄ cup	grated low-fat Cheddar cheese	175 mL
1 tsp.	dry mustard	5 mL
	salt and pepper to taste	
¹/₂ tsp.	hot pepper sauce	2 mL
1	egg, beaten	1

1. Mix flour and salt, cut in margarine and blend until mixture resembles meal.
2. Add ice water, a little at a time, until mixture is moist enough to form a firm dough. Divide dough into 15-20 balls.
3. Combine grated cheese, mustard, salt, pepper and hot pepper sauce.
4. Flatten balls into circles; place 1 tbsp. (15 mL) of cheese mixture on each circle and fold dough over to make a roll.
5. Brush rolls with beaten egg, place on a greased cookie sheet and bake at 350°F (180°C) for about 20 minutes.

Makes 15-20 rolls

1 Roll (making 15)

Energy — Calories	81	Cholesterol	22 mg
— kJ	340	Carbohydrate	7 g
Protein	2 g	Sodium	104 mg
Total Fat	5 g		

Cheese Cookies

Crunchy and spicy, these morsels are great with drinks or with soups.

²/₃ cup	**Mexican cheese spread**	**150 mL**
¹/₂ cup	**light margarine or butter**	**125 mL**
1¹/₂ cups	**flour**	**375 mL**
¹/₄ cup	**crushed nacho chips**	**60 mL**

1. Combine cheese spread with margarine, flour and nacho chips.
2. Divide mixture in half and shape into 2 rolls, about 1¹/₂" (4 cm) in diameter. Wrap tightly in plastic wrap and chill for 3 hours.
3. Slice ¹/₂" (1.3 cm) thick, place on ungreased cookie sheets and bake at 300°F (150°C) for 12-15 minutes. Serve hot.

Makes about 4-5 dozen cookies

1 Cookie (making 4 dozen)

Energy — Calories	80	**Cholesterol**	13 mg
— kJ	337	**Carbohydrate**	5 g
Protein	3 g	**Sodium**	298 mg
Total Fat	5 g		

Cheese is made from cow's, sheep's or goat's milk which is allowed to thicken until the curd separates out from the whey. Cheeses range from mild and creamy to hard and pungent and are used in appetizers, soups, salads, main courses and desserts. Cheese is a good source of protein, calcium, phosphorus, vitamins A and D and riboflavin.

Spicy Tomato Juice

Tomatoes are even more perfect with a touch of spice. Use tomato juice quickly after making it or opening the can. Oxidation causes it to lose most of its mineral content.

4 cups	tomato juice	1 L
1 tsp.	Worcestershire sauce	5 mL
1/2 tsp.	Tabasco sauce	2 mL
	juice of 1/2 lemon	
1 cup	crushed ice	250 mL
	salt to taste	

1. Combine all ingredients. Mix well and serve.

Serves 6-8

1 Serving (using 6 servings)

Energy	— Calories	29	Cholesterol	0 mg
	— kJ	117	Carbohydrate	6 g
Protein		1 g	Sodium	227 mg
Total Fat		0.3 g		

Carrot Drink

Carrot juice is enhanced by cinnamon and ginger

1 lb.	carrots, grated	500 g
2 cups	water	500 mL
	cinnamon stick	
1/2 tsp.	ground ginger	2 mL
	sugar to taste	

1. Boil grated carrots in water with cinnamon stick and ginger; simmer for about 10 minutes.

Carrot Drink

(Continued)

2. Remove cinnamon. Cool. Purée in blender.
3. Add water to desired consistency. Sweeten to taste. Refrigerate before using; keep chilled.

Serves 4

See photograph on page 17.

1 Serving

Energy — Calories	45	Cholesterol	0 mg
— kJ	186	Carbohydrate	10 g
Protein	1 g	Sodium	35 mg
Total Fat	0.2 g		

Limeade

A refreshing summer drink.

3	large limes	3
1 cup	sugar	250 mL
4 cups	water	1 L
	finely grated rind of 1 lime	
½ tsp.	Angostura bitters (optional)	2 mL

1. Cut and squeeze limes. Reserve juice.
2. Stir sugar in water until dissolved. Add rind of 1 lime.
3. Add lime juice and bitters. Stir well. Strain limeade. Chill and serve over ice.

Serves 4-6

1 Serving (using 4 servings)

Energy — Calories	235	Cholesterol	0 mg
— kJ	985	Carbohydrate	61 g
Protein	.08 g	Sodium	5 mg
Total Fat	.06 g		

Mangoade

This drink is popular in the Caribbean.

2 cups	coarsely chopped ripe mango	500 mL
1/4 cup	sugar or to taste	60 mL
1 1/2 cups	water	375 mL
1 tsp.	grated orange rind	5 mL
1 1/2 cups	orange juice	375 mL
1/2 cup	lime juice	125 mL

1. Rub the mango through a sieve.
2. Heat sugar, water and orange rind, stirring until sugar is dissolved. Cool.
3. Add sugar syrup and fruit juices to the mango purée, stirring well.
4. Refrigerate. Serve in tall glasses over ice.

Serves 6-8

See photograph on page 103.

1 Serving (using 6 servings)

Energy — Calories	74	Cholesterol	0 mg
— kJ	310	Carbohydrate	19 g
Protein	0.5 g	Sodium	6 mg
Total Fat	0.1 g		

Papaya Punch

Papaya is a good source of vitamins A, C and E and is high in calcium, phosphorus and iron.

1	medium-sized, ripe papaya	1
1 cup	1% evaporated milk	250 mL
2 cups	water	500 mL
3 tbsp.	lime juice	45 mL
1/2 tsp.	grated lime rind	2 mL
	sugar to taste	
1 cup	crushed ice	250 mL
	lime slices for garnish	

Papaya Punch

(Continued)

1. Peel papaya, cut in half and remove seeds. Mash fruit thoroughly.
2. Combine papaya, milk and water in a blender. Purée.
3. Add lime juice, lime rind and sugar; blend until mixture is smooth. Add crushed ice and blend quickly.
4. Serve in chilled glasses. Garnish with lime slices.

Serves 4-6

1 Serving (using 4 servings)

Energy	— Calories	35	Cholesterol	2 mg
	— kJ	144	Carbohydrate	5 g
Protein		2 g	Sodium	33 mg
Total Fat		0.7 g		

Cranberry Punch

2¹/₂ cups	sugar	625 mL
4 cups	water	1 L
3 cups	cranberry sauce	750 mL
¹/₂ cup	lemon juice	125 mL
8 cups	carbonated water	2 L
	ice cubes	

1. Make a syrup by boiling sugar and water together until sugar is thoroughly dissolved.
2. Add cranberry sauce, stir until smooth. Put through a sieve. Chill.
3. Stir in lemon juice.
4. When ready to serve, pour cranberry mixture over ice cubes in a punch bowl. Mix in carbonated water.

Serves 30

1 Serving

Energy	— Calories	119	Cholesterol	0 mg
	— kJ	500	Carbohydrate	31 g
Protein		.07 g	Sodium	9 mg
Total Fat		.05 g		

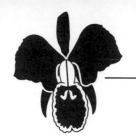

Pink Rhubarb Punch

This tart punch is refreshing and has a lovely colour.

2 lbs.	red rhubarb	1 kg
6 cups	boiling water	1.5 L
2½ cups	sugar	625 mL
3½ cups	grapefruit juice	875 mL
¼ cup	lemon juice	60 mL
4 cups	ginger ale	1 L

1. Wash rhubarb and cut into small pieces. Cook rhubarb in boiling water until it is soft, about 40 minutes. Press through a sieve.
2. Combine the rhubarb juice with sugar and stir until sugar is dissolved. Chill.
3. Add grapefruit juice and lemon juice. Chill.
4. Just before serving stir in ginger ale. Serve in tall glasses over ice.

Serves 30

1 Serving

Energy	— Calories	102	Cholesterol	0 mg
	— kJ	427	Carbohydrate	26 g
Protein		0.2 g	Sodium	3 mg
Total Fat		.05 g		

Fruit Punch

2 cups	orange juice	500 mL
2 cups	grapefruit juice	500 mL
2 cups	pineapple juice	500 mL
¼ cup	lime juice	60 mL
2¼ cups	sugar	550 mL
2 cups	water	500 mL
6 cups	ginger ale	1.5 L
	ice	
	sliced fruit	

Fruit Punch

(Continued)

1. Mix together the juices.
2. To make sugar syrup, boil sugar with water until dissolved. Cool. Add to juice mixture. Chill.
3. Before serving add chilled ginger ale and ice. Garnish with seasonal fruit.

Serves 30

1 Serving

Energy	— Calories	109	Cholesterol	0 mg
	— kJ	456	Carbohydrate	27 g
Protein		0.3 g	Sodium	4 mg
Total Fat		.04 g		

Banana-Pineapple Eggnog

This is a rich, creamy and nutritious drink.

2	eggs, beaten	2
1 cup	1% milk	250 mL
1	ripe banana	1
1 tsp.	sugar	5 mL
1/2 tsp.	vanilla essence (extract)	2 mL
2 tbsp.	pineapple juice	30 mL

1. Beat eggs and milk together. Over medium heat, cook until mixture coats the spoon. DO NOT BOIL. Remove from heat and cool.
2. Mash banana with a fork until creamy. Blend it into milk and egg mixture, add sugar, vanilla essence and pineapple juice. Chill.

Serves 4

1 Serving

Energy	— Calories	111	Cholesterol	139 mg
	— kJ	464	Carbohydrate	15 g
Protein		5 g	Sodium	66 mg
Total Fat		4 g		

Pineappleade

This delicious drink is popular in the Caribbean & Guyana.

1	medium pineapple	1
½ cup	lime juice	125 mL
2 cups	sugar	500 mL
8 cups	water	2 L

1. Peel pineapple, grate fruit finely. Place pineapple in a bowl and pour lime juice over it.
2. Boil sugar with 2 cups (500 mL) of water until dissolved. Cool.
3. Pour sugar syrup over fruit. Stir in remaining water.
4. Strain mixture pressing fruit through sieve to extract juice. Chill.
5. Serve in tall glasses over crushed ice.

Makes about 2 quarts (2 L), 10 servings

1 Serving

Energy	— Calories	211	Cholesterol	0 mg
	— kJ	881	Carbohydrate	54 g
Protein		0.2 g	Sodium	3 mg
Total Fat		0.2 g		

Sherbet

1 lb.	fruit (cherries, raspberries, mango, strawberries, pineapple or any available fruit)	500 g
3 cups	water	750 mL
	sugar to taste	
	crushed ice	

1. Crush fruit, add water and refrigerate for 6 hours.
2. Strain, discard pulp. Add sugar. Serve cold over crushed ice.

Serves 6-8

Nutritional Analysis not available because type of fruit is optional.

Soups

Avocado Soup

This cool soup is very popular in the tropical islands.

3	large, ripe avocados, chilled	3
2 cups	chilled vegetable stock, see page 46	500 mL
²/₃ cup	light, dry white wine	150 mL
²/₃ cup	10% cream	150 mL
1 tbsp.	lemon juice	15 mL
	salt and pepper to taste	
¹/₂ tsp.	cayenne pepper	2 mL
	chopped green onions	

1. Peel and purée avocados.
2. Blend in stock, wine, cream and lemon juice.
3. Add salt, pepper and cayenne. Mix well.
4. To serve, garnish with chopped green onions.

Serves 4

Note: *It is important to have all ingredients cold to prevent discolouration.*

1 Serving

Energy — Calories	373	Cholesterol	14 mg
— kJ	1563	Carbohydrate	17 g
Protein	5 g	Sodium	36 mg
Total Fat	32 g		

Avocado is low in carbohydrates and high in food energy. It is also high in iron and copper which helps to prevent anemia.

Spicy Gazpacho

The vegetables in this refreshing soup stay crisp and crunchy for a week.

2 lbs.	fresh tomatoes, peeled or 28 oz. (796 mL) canned	1 kg
1	large green pepper, seeded	1
2	garlic cloves, finely chopped	2
3/4 cup	chopped fresh mixed herbs (chives, parsley, basil, chervil, tarragon)	175 mL
1	large Spanish onion, peeled	1
1	large cucumber, peeled	1
48 oz.	tomato juice	1.36 L
1/3 cup	canola oil	75 mL
1/3 cup	lemon juice	75 mL
2 tbsp.	red wine vinegar	30 mL
2 tsp.	salt	10 mL
1/2 tsp.	paprika	2 mL
1/2 tsp.	freshly ground pepper	2 mL
2 tsp.	Worcestershire sauce or more to taste	10 mL
1/4 tsp.	Tabasco sauce or to taste	1 mL
	oil and garlic croûtons for garnish	
	chopped fresh herbs for garnish	

1. Purée tomatoes in blender; pour into a 4-quart (4 L) container.
2. Add finely chopped green pepper, garlic, herbs, onion and cucumber. Stir well. Stir in remaining ingredients, except for garnishes.
3. Cover and chill for at least 4 hours, or overnight, before serving. Garnish with croûtons, see page 33, and herbs.

Serves 10-12

1 Serving (using 10 servings)

Energy	— Calories	125	Cholesterol	0 mg
	— kJ	1053	Carbohydrate	13 g
Protein		2.7 g	Sodium	507 mg
Total Fat		8 g		

Callaloo Soup

This is a vegetarian adaptation of the famous Caribbean soup from Trinidad, Barbados, Jamaica and many other islands.

1 lb.	callaloo leaves, Chinese spinach or Swiss chard	500 g
1	celery stalk with leaves	1
3	chives or green onions, chopped	3
2	medium onions, finely chopped	2
3	garlic cloves, minced	3
1/4 tsp.	thyme	1 mL
1	sweet pepper, chopped	1
1/2 lb.	okra, sliced	250 g
1/4 tsp.	cloves	1 mL
4 cups	vegetable stock, see page 46	1 L
1 cup	coconut milk *	250 mL
	salt and pepper to taste	
1 tsp.	hot pepper sauce	5 mL

1. Wash, drain and coarsely chop greens, celery stalk and leaves. Put greens into a pot with green onions, onions, garlic, thyme, sweet pepper, okra and cloves.
2. Add vegetable stock and coconut milk. Simmer until all vegetables are soft, about 30 minutes.
3. Purée soup. Add salt, pepper and pepper sauce. Reheat. Serve hot.

Serves 6

* To make coconut milk — Grate 1 whole coconut; add 1 cup (250 mL) of warm water and let stand for 15 minutes. Strain mixture through a fine sieve, press on coconut to squeeze out all of the milk. Canned coconut milk is also available.

1 Serving

Energy — Calories	141		Cholesterol	0 mg
— kJ	591		Carbohydrate	11 g
Protein	4 g		Sodium	29 mg
Total Fat	11 g			

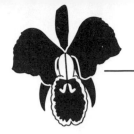

Onion Soup

Onions are prized for their flavour and nutritional value. Serve onion soup with Whole-Wheat Bread, page 97.

1 lb.	onions, chopped	500 g
3 tbsp.	light butter	45 mL
2 tbsp.	flour	30 mL
4 cups	vegetable stock, see page 46	1 L
	salt and pepper to taste	
1 cup	croûtons, see below	250 mL
4 oz.	low-fat Cheddar, grated	125 g

1. Sauté onions in butter over low heat until they are transparent. Add flour, cook, stirring for 2 minutes.
2. Bring vegetable stock to a boil. Add onion mixture, salt and pepper. Simmer for about 15 minutes.
3. Place soup in ovenproof bowls, add croûtons. Sprinkle with grated cheese; place under broiler until cheese is melted. Serve hot.

Serves 4

1 Serving (analysis includes oil and garlic croûtons)

Energy	— Calories	219	Cholesterol	42 mg
	— kJ	917	Carbohydrate	20 g
Protein		10 g	Sodium	541 mg
Total Fat		12 g		

CROÛTONS:

1. Cut any type of bread into small or large squares as you prefer.
2. Dry in a baking pan in a 250°F (120°C) oven until slightly toasted, about 20-30 minutes. Stir once or twice.
3. Store in airtight containers.
4. For **Oil and Garlic Croûtons**, toss 2 cups (500 mL) bread cubes with 1 tbsp. (15 mL) of oil. Sprinkle with minced garlic or garlic powder and toast as above.
5. For **Parmesan Garlic Croûtons**, add 2 tbsp. (30 mL) of grated Parmesan cheese to Oil and Garlic Croûtons.
6. For **Herbed Croûtons**, add chopped fresh or dried herbs to plain or Oil and Garlic Croûtons. Try parsley, oregano, dill, thyme, etc.

Chinese Vegetable Soup

This nutritious soup is very easy to prepare.

6 cups	water	1.5 L
1 cup	shredded Chinese cabbage	250 mL
½ cup	coarsely chopped tofu	125 mL
½ cup	thinly sliced mushrooms	125 mL
12	snow peas	12
⅓ cup	slivered bamboo shoots	75 mL
½ cup	sliced water chestnuts	125 mL
¼ cup	sliced carrots	60 mL
	salt and pepper to taste	

1. In a large saucepan, combine all ingredients and simmer for 15-20 minutes. Serve hot.

Serves 4-6

1 Serving (using 4 servings)

Energy — Calories	49	Cholesterol	0 mg
— kJ	205	Carbohydrate	6 g
Protein	4 g	Sodium	141 mg
Total Fat	1 g		

Mock Beef Barley

Soya cubes are a dehydrated soya bean product made from soya flour. This soup has a marvellous hearty flavour.

½ lb.	soya cubes	250 g
1 cup	water	250 mL
6 cups	vegetable stock, see page 46	1.5 L
1	large onion, chopped	1
⅔ cup	barley	150 mL
3	carrots, diced	3
2	potatoes, peeled and diced	2
2	celery stalks, diced	2
1 cup	diced turnip	250 mL
	salt and pepper to taste	

Mock Beef Barley

(Continued)

1. Soak soya cubes in 1 cup (250 mL) of water for $1/2$ hour. Cut cubes into smaller pieces.
2. In a large pot combine soya pieces, vegetable stock, onion and barley. Simmer, covered, over medium heat for about 1 hour.
3. Add carrots, potatoes, celery, turnip; simmer until tender, about 25 minutes. Season with salt and pepper. Serve hot.

Serves 8

1 Serving

Energy — Calories	197	Cholesterol	0 mg
— kJ	825	Carbohydrate	30 g
Protein	14 g	Sodium	26 mg
Total Fat	4 g		

Beet Soup

$1/2$ lb.	Betty K soya cubes	250 g
3	tomatoes, diced	3
4 cups	water	1 L
1 cup	shredded cabbage	250 mL
	salt and pepper to taste	
8	large beets, cooked, grated	8
$1/2$ cup	light sour cream	125 mL

1. Combine soya cubes, tomatoes and water, simmer, covered, for 30 minutes. Add cabbage, salt and pepper. Cook for 30 minutes.
2. Add beets; cook for 15 minutes. Serve hot. Top each serving with a spoonful of sour cream.

Serves 6-8

1 Serving (using 6 servings)

Energy — Calories	199	Cholesterol	0 mg
— kJ	832	Carbohydrate	22 g
Protein	18 g	Sodium	170 mg
Total Fat	6 g		

Pumpkin Soup

The rich smooth flavour of pumpkin is accented by hot pepper sauce. Add dumplings for a treat.

1 lb.	pumpkin, peeled and diced	500 g
1	medium onion, chopped	1
2	medium potatoes, diced	2
4 cups	water	1 L
	salt and pepper to taste	
2	green onions, chopped	2
½ tsp.	paprika	2 mL
½ tsp.	hot pepper sauce	2 mL

1. In a large saucepan combine pumpkin, onion, potatoes and water. Cover and simmer until vegetables are soft, about 30 minutes.
2. Add salt, pepper, green onions, paprika and hot pepper sauce. Simmer for a further 15 minutes. Serve hot.

Serves 4-6

1 Serving (using 4 servings)

Energy — Calories	67	Cholesterol	0 mg
— kJ	280	Carbohydrate	15 g
Protein	2 g	Sodium	7 mg
Total Fat	0.4 g		

Dumplings

2 cups	flour	500 mL
1 tbsp.	baking powder	15 mL
2 tbsp.	light butter	30 mL
½ tsp.	salt	2 mL
	cold water	

1. Mix flour with baking powder, butter and salt.
2. Add enough cold water to make a fairly stiff dough.
3. Shape dough into balls about 1" (2.5 cm) in diameter, then flatten. Drop into soup; cover and cook for about 10 minutes.

Makes about 12-14 dumplings

Dumplings

(Continued)

1 Dumpling

Energy	— Calories	95	Cholesterol	0 mg
	— kJ	395	Carbohydrate	18 g
Protein		3 g	Sodium	233 mg
Total Fat		1 g		

Mushroom Soup

The curry adds a spicy touch to this creamy soup.

1	small onion, chopped	1
4	green onions, chopped	4
1 tbsp.	light butter	15 mL
1/2 tsp.	curry powder	2 mL
1/2 lb.	mushrooms, minced	250 g
1 cup	water	250 mL
2 tbsp.	flour	30 mL
2 cups	1% milk	500 mL
	salt and pepper to taste	
1/4 cup	10% cream	60 mL
	chives and parsley sprigs	

1. Sauté onions and green onions in butter until soft. Add curry powder and mushrooms. Stir. Add water and bring to a boil.
2. Blend flour and milk, pour into mushroom mixture with salt and pepper, simmer until thickened, about 30 minutes.
3. Stir in cream. Heat but do not boil. Garnish with chopped chives and parsley.

Serves 4

1 Serving

Energy	— Calories	122	Cholesterol	11 mg
	— kJ	510	Carbohydrate	14 g
Protein		7 g	Sodium	95 mg
Total Fat		5 g		

Corn Soup

This creamy corn soup has a smooth full-bodied flavour.

½ lb.	Betty K soya cubes	250 g
2 cups	water	500 mL
1	small onion, chopped	1
1	garlic clove, minced	1
1 tbsp.	vegetable oil	15 mL
3 cups	1% milk	750 mL
4 cups	creamed corn	1 L
1 tbsp.	light butter	15 mL
	salt and pepper to taste	

1. Soak soya cubes in 1 cup (250 mL) water for about ½ hour. Cut into small pieces.
2. In a large saucepan, sauté onions and garlic in hot oil, add soya pieces, cook until brown. Add 1 cup (250 mL) water and bring to a boil. Cover and simmer for about 45 minutes.
3. Stir in milk, creamed corn, butter, salt and pepper. Mix well. Simmer for 10 minutes. Serve hot.

Serves 6-8

1 Serving (using 6 servings)

Energy	— Calories	345	Cholesterol	5 mg
	— kJ	1443	Carbohydrate	49 g
Protein		22 g	Sodium	550 mg
Total Fat		10 g		

Corn is native to North and South America. It is very high in fibre and magnesium. It is also rich in carbohydrates. The yellow kernels contain vitamin A and it is also a source of potassium, niacin and protein. Corn aids in elimination.

Chunky Corn Chowder

Spicy and rich flavoured, this hearty soup needs only a salad and whole-wheat bread to make a satisfying meal.

6 cups	vegetable stock, page 46	1.5 L
4	large potatoes, peeled and diced	4
2	medium onions, finely chopped	2
1	large garlic clove, minced	1
1/2 tsp.	thyme	2 mL
1/2 tsp.	crushed red pepper	2 mL
2x19 oz.	cans niblets corn	2x540 mL
1-2 tsp.	hot pepper sauce, page 18 of *Caribbean Cuisine* or use bottled sauce	5-10 mL
2 cups	1% milk	500 mL

1. In a large saucepan, bring stock to a boil. Add potatoes, onions and seasonings. Cover and reduce heat. Simmer for 20-30 minutes, until potatoes are tender.
2. Add corn and pepper sauce. Simmer for 10 minutes.
3. Add milk and heat through. Serve hot.

Serves 10

1 Serving

Energy — Calories	162	Cholesterol	2 mg
— kJ	677	Carbohydrate	35 g
Protein	6 g	Sodium	44 mg
Total Fat	2 g		

Thyme is native to the Mediterranean area and southern Europe. It is a member of the mint family. There are several varieties including lemon thyme which has a stronger lemon aroma than the garden thyme usually used in cooking.

Cheese Soup

Cheddar cheese adds a hearty tang to chunky vegetable soup.

3 cups	peeled, chopped potatoes	750 mL
1/2 cup	finely sliced celery	125 mL
1/2 cup	finely diced carrots	125 mL
1/4 cup	chopped onion	60 mL
1 tbsp.	chopped fresh parsley	15 mL
1 cup	vegetable stock, page 46	250 mL
	salt and pepper to taste	
1 1/2 cups	1% milk	375 mL
2 tbsp.	flour	30 mL
1 1/2 cups	grated low-fat Cheddar cheese	375 mL

1. In a large pot, combine potatoes, celery, carrots, onion, parsley, vegetable stock, salt and pepper; bring to a boil. Cover and simmer for 20 minutes.
2. Add milk to flour and blend; pour into vegetable mixture and cook, stirring until thickened.
3. Add grated cheese, stir until melted. Serve hot.

Serves 4

1 Serving

Energy	— Calories	216	Cholesterol	67 mg
	— kJ	906	Carbohydrate	31 g
Protein		16 g	Sodium	400 mg
Total Fat		4 g		

Celery is native to Europe and Northern Africa. It was prized as a medicinal herb. Celery is high in fibre and low in calories. The greener stalks are a good source of vitamin A. It is also a good source of vitamin B, potassium and magnesium.

Split Pea Soup

Serve this delicious soup with whole-grain bread.

8 oz.	yellow split peas	250 g
4 cups	water	1 L
1	small onion, chopped	1
1	garlic clove, minced	1
	salt and pepper to taste	
¼ lb.	carrots, diced	125 g
1	celery stalk, diced	1
2 tsp.	flour	5 mL
¼ cup	1% milk	60 mL

1. In a large saucepan, combine peas, water, onions, garlic, salt and pepper. Bring to a boil and simmer until peas are soft, about 45 minutes.
2. Purée pea mixture in blender. Reheat puréed mixture, add carrots and celery and simmer until vegetables are tender, about 20 minutes.
3. Blend flour and milk and add to soup. Simmer for 5 minutes. Serve hot.

Serves 4-6

1 Serving

Energy — Calories	222	Cholesterol	0.6 mg
— kJ	930	Carbohydrate	41 g
Protein	15 g	Sodium	45 mg
Total Fat	0.8 g		

Split peas or field peas are part of the bean family. They are a very good protein source, containing more than meat, eggs or fish and approximately double the amount of whole-grain cereals.

Lentil Soup

Pasta adds a touch of Italy to this lentil soup.

2 tbsp.	vegetable oil	30 mL
3	large garlic cloves, minced	3
1	onion, minced	1
1/2 cup	dry lentils	125 mL
4 cups	vegetable stock, see page 46	1 L
28 oz.	can tomatoes	796 mL
3	carrots, sliced	3
2	celery stalks, diced	2
1 cup	pasta shells	250 mL
1	zucchini, sliced	1
1/4 cup	chopped green onions	60 mL
	salt and pepper to taste	
1/2 tsp.	Betty K. seasoning or seasoned salt	2 mL

1. In a large saucepan heat oil, sauté garlic and onion until soft. Add lentils and cook for about 3 minutes.
2. Stir in vegetable stock, tomatoes with juice, bring to a boil. Simmer, covered, for about 35 minutes, stirring occasionally.
3. Add carrots, celery and pasta; simmer until pasta is tender.
4. Stir in zucchini and green onions; add salt, pepper and Betty K seasoning to taste, simmer for 2 minutes. Serve hot.

Serves 6

See photograph on page 51.

1 Serving

Energy	— Calories	240	Cholesterol	0 mg
	— kJ	1004	Carbohydrate	40 g
Protein		9 g	Sodium	371 mg
Total Fat		5 g		

The European or Chinese lentil varies from brown to green. The Indian or Egyptian lentil is red. They are a good source of iron and phosphorus, a fair source of Vitamins A, B plus calcium.

Hearty Spicy Lentil Soup

Rich and peppery, this soup is filling, perfect for a cold winter day.

6 cups	vegetable stock, page 46	1.5 L
2 cups	dry lentils or 2 x 19 oz. (2 x 540 mL) cans lentils	500 mL
2	onions, finely chopped	2
3	large ripe tomatoes, peeled and chopped	3
4	garlic cloves, minced	4
4	medium carrots, quartered and sliced	4
1 tsp.	thyme	5 mL
1/2 tsp.	savory	2 mL
1-2 tsp.	ground ginger	5-10 mL
1 tbsp.	crushed cumin seeds	15 mL
1 tsp.	paprika	5 mL
1/2-1 tsp.	cayenne pepper	2-5 mL
1-2 tsp.	hot pepper sauce, see page 18 of *Caribbean Cuisine* or use bottled sauce	5-10 mL
	salt and pepper to taste	

1. In a large saucepan, combine all ingredients. Cover and bring to a boil. Reduce heat and simmer for 1 hour.
2. For a thicker soup, remove 1 cup (250 mL) of vegetables and lentils from soup and purée. Return purée to soup. Heat and serve.

Serves 8-10

Variation: *Add 2-3 diced potatoes and/or 1 cup (250 mL) small pasta shells if you wish. Add pasta for last 20 minutes.*

1 Serving (using 8 servings)

Energy	— Calories	207	Cholesterol	0 mg
	— kJ	866	Carbohydrate	38 g
Protein		14 g	Sodium	37 mg
Total Fat		0.9 g		

43

Black Bean Soup

Here is a vegetarian variation of a popular island soup.

2 cups	dried black beans	500 mL
3 cups	water	750 mL
1	onion, chopped	1
2	garlic cloves, minced	2
1 tbsp.	minced fresh ginger	15 mL
¼ cup	chopped green onions	60 mL
½ tsp.	dried thyme	2 mL
1	sprig of parsley	1
1	bay leaf	1
2	celery stalks, sliced	2
6 cups	vegetable stock, see page 46	1.5 L

1. Soak the beans in cold water overnight.
2. Drain beans, discard water and place black beans in a large saucepan.
3. Add onions, garlic, ginger, green onions, thyme, parsley, bay leaf, celery and vegetable stock. Simmer for about 2 hours.
4. Discard bay leaf. Purée soup until smooth. Reheat. Serve hot.

Serves 6

1 Serving

Energy — Calories	232	Cholesterol	0 mg
— kJ	969	Carbohydrate	43 g
Protein	15 g	Sodium	15 mg
Total Fat	0.7 g		

Black beans are also called Turtle beans. Used in soups, stews and casseroles, they are also used to grow bean sprouts. Like other dried beans, they are rich in protein, iron, calcium and phosphorus.

Chickpea Mulligatawny

Chickpeas replace chicken in this peppery East Indian soup.

2 tbsp.	oil	30 mL
2	onions, finely chopped	2
4-5	garlic cloves, minced	4-5
4	celery stalks, thinly sliced	4
4	carrots, quartered and sliced	4
2	large potatoes, peeled and diced	2
2x19 oz.	cans of chickpeas, drained	2x540 mL
2 cups	uncooked rice	500 mL
1/2 tsp.	crushed red pepper	2 mL
1 tsp.	cayenne pepper	5 mL
3-4 tsp.	curry powder, see page 19 in *Caribbean Cuisine* or use commercial powder	15-20 mL
1/2 tsp.	ground ginger	2 mL
1 tsp.	each salt and pepper or more to taste	5 mL
10 cups	vegetable stock, page 46	2.5 L
1 cup	plain yogurt or 10% cream (optional)	250 mL

1. In a large saucepan, heat oil and add vegetables, rice and seasonings. Stir-fry until onions are translucent, 4-5 minutes.
2. Add vegetable stock, cover and bring to a boil. Reduce heat and simmer for 20-30 minutes, until rice is cooked and vegetables are tender.
3. Stir in yogurt or cream, if you wish. Reheat soup and serve hot.

Serves 10-12

1 Serving (using 10 servings)

Energy	— Calories	323	Cholesterol	4 mg
	— kJ	1350	Carbohydrate	60 g
Protein		10 g	Sodium	25 mg
Total Fat		5 g		

Vegetable Stock

This basic stock can be used in place of chicken, beef or fish stock in many soup recipes.

1	large onion, peeled, chopped	1
2	carrots, peeled, sliced	2
2	celery stalks with leaves, chopped	2
1 tsp.	thyme	5 mL
1 tbsp.	chopped parsley	15 mL
1 tsp.	dill seed (optional)	5 mL
2	bay leaves	2
1/2 tsp.	freshly ground pepper	2 mL
3 qts.	water	3 L

1. In a large saucepan, combine all ingredients. Bring to a boil over medium heat. Keep at a gentle boil for 50-60 minutes.
2. Skim off foam as it rises to the surface.
3. Strain and refrigerate or freeze until needed.

Makes about 10 cups (2.5 L)

Bay leaves or laurel leaves were used by the Greeks and Romans who considered them to have magical properties. Laurel wreaths were awarded to victors in sporting and military contests. Turkish bay leaves have a subtle flavour and 1-2" (2.5-5 cm) long oval leaves. California bay leaves have 2-3" (5-7 cm) long narrow leaves.

Salads

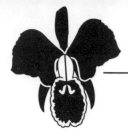

Papaya Salad

This lovely combination of flavours needs no salad dressing.

1	medium, firm papaya	1
1	small, ripe pineapple, peeled and diced	1
2	green onions, finely diced	2
1	apple, peeled and diced	1
1/2 cup	thinly sliced celery	125 mL
1	small, firm mango, peeled and diced	
	salt and pepper to taste	
1 tbsp.	lemon juice	15 mL

1. Peel papaya. Cut in 1/2 and scoop out seeds.
2. Dice papaya and combine with remaining ingredients.
3. Cover and chill before serving.

Serves 6-8

1 Serving (using 6 servings)

Energy — Calories	32		Cholesterol	0 mg
— kJ	135		Carbohydrate	8 g
Protein	0.3 g		Sodium	7 mg
Total Fat	0.2 g			

Green Banana Salad

Green banana is very popular in Jamaica.

2 lbs.	very green bananas	1 kg
	water	
2 tsp.	oil	10 mL
1	medium cucumber	1
1	sweet pepper, seeded	1
1	onion, chopped	1
2 tbsp.	lime juice	30 mL
1 tsp.	salt	5 mL
1 tsp.	hot pepper sauce	5 mL

Green Banana Salad

(Continued)

1. Boil bananas with skins on in enough water to cover bananas. Add oil to water to prevent the sticky substance from the banana skins clinging to pot.
2. Cook until tender, about 30 minutes. Let bananas cool; peel them.
3. Peel cucumber, slice thinly, add thinly sliced pepper, onion, lime juice, salt and hot pepper sauce. Combine.
4. Slice bananas into 1" (2.5 cm) pieces, add to cucumber mixture, mixing well. Marinate for 1 hour before serving.

Serves 6

1 Serving

Energy — Calories	194	**Cholesterol**	0 mg
— kJ	813	**Carbohydrate**	49 g
Protein	2 g	**Sodium**	325 mg
Total Fat	1 g		

Cucumber Salad

2	cucumbers	2
1 tsp.	salt	5 mL
¼ cup	white vinegar	60 mL
¼ cup	sugar	60 mL
1	garlic clove, minced	1
½ tsp.	paprika	2 mL
¼ cup	natural yogurt	60 mL

1. Slice unpeeled cucumber, add salt and let sit for ½ hour. Drain.
2. Mix vinegar, sugar, garlic and paprika; add cucumbers and toss.
3. Add yogurt to cucumber mixture; stir. Chill for 2-3 hours. Serve.

Serves 4-6

1 Serving (using 4 servings)

Energy — Calories	73	**Cholesterol**	.08 mg
— kJ	304	**Carbohydrate**	18 g
Protein	0.8 g	**Sodium**	493 mg
Total Fat	0.1 g		

Creole Salad

Creole cooking represents the best elements of Spanish, French and African cuisines. This colourful salad will keep well up to 2 days.

2	red peppers, cored and seeded	2
2	green peppers, cored and seeded	2
1	onion, thinly sliced	1
2	celery stalks, finely chopped	2
2	tomatoes, cut in wedges	2
1/4 cup	sliced green olives	60 mL
1/4 cup	sliced black olives	60 mL
1/4 cup	vegetable oil	60 mL
2 tbsp.	white vinegar	30 mL
1	garlic clove, minced	1
1 tsp.	dried basil	5 mL
	salt and pepper to taste	
1/2 tsp.	Betty K seasoning	2 mL
1 tsp.	sugar	5 mL

1. Chop peppers into 1/2" (1.3 cm) pieces. Add onion, celery, tomatoes and olives.
2. Mix together oil, vinegar, garlic, basil, salt, pepper, seasoning and sugar.
3. Pour over vegetables and toss gently.
4. Cover and refrigerate for a few hours before serving.

Serves 4

See photograph opposite.

1 Serving

Energy	— Calories	209	Cholesterol	0 mg
	— kJ	876	Carbohydrate	14 g
Protein		2 g	Sodium	886 mg
Total Fat		18 g		

Soup and Salad

Oriental Radish Salad

Radishes originated in China so this flavourful salad is very authentic.

12	radishes	12
1	small green pepper, seeded	1
¹/₂ cup	Betty K soya cubes, cooked *	125 mL

DRESSING:

3 tbsp.	vegetable oil	45 mL
2 tsp.	soy sauce	10 mL
1 tsp.	sugar	5 mL
	salt and pepper to taste	
¹/₂ tsp.	Betty K seasoning	2 mL

1. Slice radishes thinly. Chop green pepper and cut cooked soya cubes into bite-sized pieces. Mix.
2. Combine vegetable oil, soy sauce, sugar, salt, pepper and Betty K seasoning.
3. Toss vegetables and soya cubes with dressing. Cover and refrigerate for several hours. Serve on a bed of lettuce or in a hollowed-out crusty roll.

Serves 2

* To cook soya cubes — Boil 2 oz. (55 g) of soya cubes in 1 cup (250 mL) of water for about 15 minutes, until tender and water is absorbed. When cold this measures 1 cup (250 mL).

1 Serving

Energy — Calories	318	Cholesterol	0 mg
— kJ	1329	Carbohydrate	16 g
Protein	13 g	Sodium	796 mg
Total Fat	24 g		

Kutchumber

This combination of tomatoes and cucumber makes a delicious side dish.

1	cucumber, peeled and diced	1
2	tomatoes, sliced	2
2	onions, finely chopped	2
4	lettuce leaves, shredded	4
1 tbsp.	vinegar	15 mL
1 tbsp.	lime juice	15 mL
	salt and pepper to taste	
1/4 tsp.	chili powder	1 mL
1 tsp.	Betty K. seasoning	5 mL

1. Combine cucumber, tomatoes, onions and lettuce.
2. In a separate bowl, combine vinegar, lime juice, salt, pepper, chili powder and seasoning. Add to cucumber mixture and toss.
3. Refrigerate, covered, for 2-3 hours before serving.

Serves 3-4

1 Serving (using 3 servings)

Energy — Calories	47	Cholesterol	0 mg
— kJ	198	Carbohydrate	10 g
Protein	2 g	Sodium	661 mg
Total Fat	0.5 g		

Cucumbers were originally native to India or Thailand. They are nonstarchy and alkaline. They have a cooling effect when eaten with spicy foods and many people recognize them as beneficial to digestion.

Zucchini Salad

Colour and flavour make this a favourite warm weather salad.

2 cups	thinly sliced zucchini	500 mL
1 cup	sliced mushrooms	250 mL
1 cup	halved cherry tomatoes	250 mL
2 tbsp.	chopped parsley	30 mL
1/2 cup	thinly sliced purple onions	125 mL
	Creamy Tofu Dressing, see below	
4-6 cups	shredded lettuce	1-1.5 L

1. Combine all vegetables, except for lettuce, in a bowl.
2. Pour dressing over vegetables and mix. Refrigerate for several hours. Serve over shredded lettuce.

Serves 4-6

CREAMY TOFU DRESSING:

6 oz.	tofu, pressed	170 g
2 tbsp.	lemon juice	30 mL
2 tbsp.	vegetable oil	30 mL
	salt and pepper to taste	

1. Blend all ingredients in a blender.

See photograph on page 85.

1 Serving (using 4 servings)

Energy — Calories	120	Cholesterol	0 mg
— kJ	500	Carbohydrate	8 g
Protein	5 g	Sodium	9 mg
Total Fat	9 g		

Mixed Bean Salad

Chickpeas are deservedly very popular in India, the Mediterranean area and the Middle East.

19 oz.	can chickpeas, drained	540 mL
19 oz.	can kidney beans, drained	540 mL
1 cup	diced cucumber	250 mL
2	celery stalks, sliced	2
1	small onion, thinly sliced	1
3/4 cup	natural yogurt	175 mL
1 tsp.	lemon juice	5 mL
2 tsp.	ground cumin	10 mL
2	garlic cloves, minced	2
1 tsp.	Betty K seasoning	5 mL
1/4 cup	chopped parsley	60 mL

1. Combine chickpeas, beans, cucumber, celery and onion.
2. Combine yogurt, lemon juice, cumin, garlic and Betty K seasoning.
3. Toss bean mixture with dressing. Sprinkle with parsley. Cover and refrigerate. Serve cold.

Serves 6

1 Serving

Energy	— Calories	156	Cholesterol	3 mg
	— kJ	654	Carbohydrate	27 g
Protein		9 g	Sodium	344 mg
Total Fat		2 g		

Coleslaw

4 cups	shredded cabbage	1 L
3/4 cup	shredded carrots	175 mL
1/2 cup	chopped walnuts	125 mL
1/2 cup	light mayonnaise	125 mL
2 tbsp.	sugar	30 mL
1 tbsp.	cider vinegar	15 mL
1 tbsp.	Betty K seasoning	15 mL

Coleslaw

(Continued)

1. Combine cabbage, carrots and nuts in a bowl.
2. Combine mayonnaise, sugar, vinegar and seasoning. Spoon over cabbage mixture. Toss well. Cover and chill before serving.

Serves 4-6

1 Serving (using 4 servings)

Energy	— Calories	225	Cholesterol	0 mg
	— kJ	941	Carbohydrate	23 g
Protein		3 g	Sodium	1484 mg
Total Fat		15 g		

Red Cabbage Slaw

½	medium red cabbage	½
2	red-skinned apples	2
1	onion, thinly sliced	1
½ cup	coarsely chopped parsley	125 mL

DRESSING:

½ cup	vegetable oil	125 mL
2 tbsp.	red wine vinegar	30 mL
1 tbsp.	sugar	15 mL
½ tsp.	caraway seeds	2 mL
	salt and pepper to taste	

1. Finely shred cabbage, cut unpeeled, cored apples into thin slices; mix with sliced onions and parsley.
2. Blend salad dressing ingredients. Pour dressing over cabbage mixture; toss. Cover and refrigerate for several hours.

Serves 4

1 Serving

Energy	— Calories	333	Cholesterol	0 mg
	— kJ	1394	Carbohydrate	22 g
Protein		2 g	Sodium	29 mg
Total Fat		28 g		

Peppery Rice Salad

Delicious and hot, this recipe comes from Vietnam. It was given to me by a friend.

2 cups	uncooked rice	500 mL
1	hot pepper, finely chopped	1
1	small red onion, thinly sliced	1
1	red pepper, cut in strips	1
1	green pepper, cut in strips	1
1/2 lb.	spinach leaves, shredded	250 g
1	head of lettuce, shredded	1
1/2 cup	cider vinegar	125 mL
2 tsp.	soy sauce	10 mL
2 tbsp.	lemon juice	30 mL
1 tsp.	liquid honey	5 mL
2 cups	bean sprouts	500 mL

1. Rinse rice before cooking to make it less sticky. Cook rice according to package directions. Let stand, covered, for 5 minutes; fluff with a fork.
2. Place rice in a bowl, stir in hot pepper, red onion, red pepper, green pepper, spinach and lettuce.
3. Prepare dressing by mixing vinegar, soy sauce, lemon juice and honey. Keep at room temperature.
4. Just before serving, toss with salad dressing until the rice is well coated. Gently stir in bean sprouts. Serve warm or at room temperature.

Serves 6-8

See photograph on front cover.

1 Serving (using 6 servings)

Energy — Calories	219	Cholesterol	0 mg
— kJ	916	Carbohydrate	48 g
Protein	6 g	Sodium	164 mg
Total Fat	0.6 g		

New Potato Salad

The flavours of new potatoes and red peppers are complemented by a lemon yogurt dressing.

4 cups	quartered new potatoes	1 L
2 tbsp.	minced red onions	30 mL
2 tbsp.	minced sweet red peppers	30 mL
1/4 cup	low-fat yogurt	60 mL
2 tbsp.	lemon juice	30 mL
1/4 tsp.	dried basil	1 mL
1/2 tsp.	honey	2 mL
1/4 tsp.	dry mustard	1 mL
	red pepper and red onion rings to garnish	

1. In a large pot of water, boil the potatoes until tender, about 15-20 minutes.
2. Combine onions and peppers in a serving bowl.
3. Blend together yogurt, lemon juice, basil, honey and mustard.
4. Add drained, cooked potatoes to the onion mixture, pour on dressing and toss gently. Serve hot or cold. Garnish with sweet red pepper and onion rings.

Serves 4-6

1 Serving (using 4 servings)

Energy — Calories	100	Cholesterol	.08 mg
— kJ	420	Carbohydrate	23 g
Protein	3 g	Sodium	12 mg
Total Fat	0.2 g		

Sweet red bell peppers are vine-ripened green bell peppers. They are both good sources of vitamin C and also contain vitamins A and B plus some calcium, phosphorus and iron.

Spicy Potato Salad

Cumin, chilis and garlic add zest to this version of a universal favourite.

3	potatoes, boiled and cubed	3
1 tbsp.	ground cumin	15 mL
1	green chili pepper, finely chopped	1
2	garlic cloves, minced	2
1	onion, finely chopped	1
1 tbsp.	light butter	15 mL
	salt and pepper	
½ cup	light mayonnaise	125 mL
	chopped green onions for garnish	

1. Place cubed potatoes in a bowl.
2. Stir-fry cumin powder in a small frying pan until browned and aromatic; sprinkle over potatoes.
3. Sauté green chili, garlic and onion in butter; pour over potatoes.
4. Mix in salt, pepper and mayonnaise. Chill. Garnish with chopped green onions before serving.

Serves 3-4

1 Serving (using 3 servings)

Energy	— Calories	236	Cholesterol	0 mg
	— kJ	989	Carbohydrate	29 g
Protein		3 g	Sodium	193 mg
Total Fat		13 g		

Valued for its medicinal and flavouring properties for centuries, garlic was native to the Mediterranean and Western Asia. It is a member of the lily family. There are several varieties of garlic. The Creole of America is the strongest flavoured and has a white skin. The Italian or Mexican has smaller cloves and a pink skin.

Russian Salad

Pineapple adds a refreshing flavour to this vegetable salad.

2	potatoes, boiled and diced	2
3	carrots, boiled and sliced	3
1 cup	steamed chopped green beans	250 mL
1 cup	steamed peas	250 mL
1	celery stalk, chopped	1
	salt and pepper to taste	
¼ cup	light mayonnaise	60 mL
1 cup	sugar-free pineapple tidbits	250 mL

1. Combine potatoes, carrots, beans, peas and celery.
2. Blend salt, pepper and mayonnaise. Mix with vegetables.
3. Add pineapple. Chill for 3-4 hours and serve.

Serves 4

1 Serving

Energy	— Calories	185	Cholesterol	0 mg
	— kJ	773	Carbohydrate	35 g
Protein		4 g	Sodium	202 mg
Total Fat		4 g		

Pineapples are native to the Caribbean and Central America. They are a good source of potassium, high in vitamin C and also contain some iron. They help to digest proteins and are used to aid digestion and elimination.

Macaroni Salad

This pasta salad is portable and flavourful. Try shells and spirals for variety.

2 cups	cooked macaroni	500 mL
1	onion, chopped	1
1	cucumber, diced	1
1/2 cup	chopped parsley	125 mL
1/4 cup	vegetable oil	60 mL
1/4 cup	lemon juice	60 mL
1/2 tsp.	sugar	2 mL
1	garlic clove, crushed	1
1/2 tsp.	dry mustard	2 mL
	salt and pepper to taste	
1/2 tsp.	Betty K seasoning	2 mL

1. Combine macaroni, onion, cucumber and parsley.
2. In a blender, blend vegetable oil, lemon juice, sugar, garlic, dry mustard, salt, pepper and Betty K seasoning.
3. Pour dressing over macaroni mixture and toss. Chill for 3-4 hours before serving.

Serves 4-6

1 Serving (using 4 servings)

Energy	— Calories	199	Cholesterol	0 mg
	— kJ	834	Carbohydrate	17 g
Protein		3 g	Sodium	250 mg
Total Fat		14 g		

There are many varieties of parsley including a European version that has a turnip-like root and is cooked like a root vegetable. The curly-leafed and Italian or flat-leafed parsley are the most popular. Parsley is a good source of vitamins A and C, iron, copper and manganese. It is used as a blood purifier and diuretic, and it stimulates the bowels.

Side Dishes
&
Main Courses

Curried Cauliflower

Serve this tasty dish on a bed of rice.

1	onion, chopped	1
2	garlic cloves, minced	2
2 tbsp.	vegetable oil	30 mL
2 tsp.	curry powder	10 mL
1	medium cauliflower*, in florets	1
1/2 tsp.	paprika	2 mL
1/2 tsp.	chili powder	2 mL
1/2 tsp.	cumin powder	2 mL
	salt and pepper to taste	
1/2 cup	water	125 mL

1. Sauté onion and garlic in vegetable oil until translucent, add curry powder; sauté for 1 minute.
2. Stir cauliflower into onion mixture.
3. Add paprika, chili, cumin, salt and pepper. Cover and cook slowly for about 10 minutes. Add water and simmer for about 15 minutes, until cauliflower is tender.

Serves 4

* *Cabbage pieces, diced pumpkin, eggplant slices or potato pieces may be used.*

1 Serving

Energy	— Calories	93	Cholesterol	0 mg
	— kJ	390	Carbohydrate	7 g
Protein		2 g	Sodium	15 mg
Total Fat		7 g		

Cauliflower is a member of the cabbage family. It is high in vitamin C and is a fair source of iron. The leaves contain calcium and they can be cooked with the head or used in salads. For diabetics, it is easier to digest than cabbage. It is also very low in calories.

Spicy Roast Potatoes

These potatoes are colourful and have a wonderful aroma and flavour.

1 lb.	potatoes, peeled	500 g
1	onion, diced	1
2 tbsp.	light butter	30 mL
1 tsp.	paprika	5 mL
1/2 tsp.	chili powder	2 mL
1/2 tsp.	Garam Masala, page 20 of *Caribbean Cuisine* or use a commercial mixture	2 mL
1/2 tsp.	Betty K seasoning	2 mL

1. Parboil potatoes until partially cooked, about 10-15 minutes.
2. Sauté onion in butter, add paprika, chili powder, garam masala and Betty K seasoning.
3. Toss potatoes in seasoning mixture. Transfer to ovenproof dish, cover and bake at 350°F (180°C) for about 30 minutes.

Serves 4

1 Serving

Energy	— Calories	127	Cholesterol	0 mg
	— kJ	531	Carbohydrate	23 g
Protein		3 g	Sodium	299 mg
Total Fat		3 g		

Potatoes were native to tropical America. They are not high in calories and are virtually a complete food. Potatoes are high in vitamins C and B-6 and in potassium as well as low in sodium. Leave the peel on potatoes whenever possible. Sixty percent of the potassium is removed by peeling and if the peels are retained you won't have to salt the potatoes. Potatoes are a good source of minerals and complex carbohydrates.

Sliced Baked Potatoes

Cumin and 2 cheeses add a rich flavour to this dish.

4	medium potatoes	4
1 tsp.	Betty K seasoning	5 mL
1 tbsp.	chopped parsley	15 mL
1 tbsp.	chopped green onions	15 mL
1 tbsp.	ground cumin	15 mL
2 tbsp.	melted light butter	30 mL
4 tbsp.	grated low-fat Cheddar cheese	60 mL
2 tbsp.	grated Parmesan cheese	30 mL

1. Scrub potatoes and rinse. Slice potatoes thinly, not all the way through.
2. Put potatoes in a baking dish, fan them slightly.
3. Sprinkle with Betty K seasoning, parsley, green onions and cumin. Drizzle melted butter over potatoes.
4. Bake potatoes at 375°F (190°C) for about 50 minutes. Remove from oven. Sprinkle with Cheddar and Parmesan cheese.
5. Bake for another 15 minutes, until lightly browned, cheese is melted and potatoes are cooked. Serve with a salad.

Serves 4

1 Serving

Energy — Calories	137	Cholesterol	4 mg
— kJ	571	Carbohydrate	20 g
Protein	5 g	Sodium	633 mg
Total Fat	4 g		

Cumin, also called comino, is the dried seed of a member of the parsley family. It comes in white, amber and black and has a nutty flavour. The black has a more peppery flavour. It is used in Asian, Middle Eastern and Mediterranean cooking and to make curries and chili powders.

Potato/Vegetable Pie

Try your favourite vegetable combinations in this versatile potato crust pie.

2 cups	cooked potatoes	500 mL
2 tbsp.	light butter	30 mL
1/4 cup	1% milk	60 mL
1/2 cup	flour	125 mL
1/3 tsp.	baking powder	1.5 mL
	salt and pepper to taste	
1/4 cup	grated low-fat Cheddar cheese	60 mL

FILLING:

1 tbsp.	vegetable oil	15 mL
1	onion, chopped	1
1	garlic clove, minced	1
1	pkg. spinach leaves, chopped or any vegetable of choice	1
1/4 tsp.	paprika	1 mL
1 tsp.	hot pepper sauce	5 mL
	salt and pepper to taste	
	butter for topping	

1. Mash potatoes, butter and milk, when cool add flour, baking powder, salt and pepper. Mix into a soft dough.
2. Line a greased 9" (23 cm) pie plate with half of dough. Sprinkle with 1/2 of grated cheese.
3. To prepare filling, heat oil, sauté onion and garlic until soft. Add chopped spinach or other vegetable, paprika, hot pepper sauce, salt and pepper. Cook until tender. Spread over dough in pie plate.
4. Cover filling with remaining dough. Sprinkle with remaining cheese, dot with butter. Bake at 350°F (180°C) for 30 minutes.

Serves 6

1 Serving

Energy — Calories	180	Cholesterol	2 mg
— kJ	753	Carbohydrate	29 g
Protein	6 g	Sodium	140 mg
Total Fat	5 g		

Tomatoes Stuffed with Spinach

Garam Masala adds a fresh curry flavour to this substantial tomato dish.

4	large tomatoes	4
2 tbsp.	vegetable oil	30 mL
1	small onion, chopped	1
2	garlic cloves, minced	2
1 tsp.	turmeric	5 mL
1 tsp.	Garam Masala, page 20, *Caribbean Cuisine*	5 mL
2 tsp.	paprika	10 mL
12 oz.	spinach, fresh or frozen	340 g
½ cup	mashed potato	125 mL
	salt and pepper to taste	

1. Wash tomatoes, carefully cut off the top; scoop out seeds and pulp, reserve.
2. Heat oil, sauté onion and garlic, adding turmeric, garam masala and paprika, stirring frequently.
3. Chop spinach finely. Mix it with mashed potato, tomato pulp, salt and pepper. Add to onion mixture, cook for 5 minutes. Cool.
4. Place filling in tomato shells, replace lids. Bake in a covered dish at 375°F (190°C) for 15-20 minutes. Serve over hot rice.

Serves 4

1 Serving

Energy — Calories	143	Cholesterol	0.5 mg
— kJ	599	Carbohydrate	16 g
Protein	5 g	Sodium	148 mg
Total Fat	9 g		

Native to South America, the tomato is a very valuable fruit. It is high in vitamins C , A and B, potassium, iron and phosphorous. Like the potato and the eggplant, it is a member of the nightshade family and it was thought to be poisonous.

Baked Stuffed Eggplant

A tasty entrée, the soya mince adds an interesting texture.

1 lb.	eggplant	500 g
1	onion, chopped	1
1	garlic clove, minced	1
2 tbsp.	light butter	30 mL
1/4 lb.	Betty K soya mince	125 g
	salt and pepper to taste	
1 tsp.	hot pepper sauce	5 mL
1/4 cup	water	60 mL
1 tbsp.	chopped green onions	15 mL
2 tbsp.	bread crumbs	30 mL
2 tbsp.	grated Parmesan cheese	30 mL

1. Boil unpeeled eggplant until tender, about 15 minutes.
2. Cut eggplant in half lengthwise; carefully remove pulp, mash until smooth. Retain skin.
3. Sauté onion and garlic in 1 tbsp. (15 mL) of butter; add soya mince, salt, pepper and hot pepper sauce. Sauté for about 5 minutes. Add water, bring to a boil; when water is absorbed, remove from heat.
4. Add eggplant pulp and green onions to soya mixture. Mix well. Return filling to eggplant skin.
5. Place in a baking pan. Sprinkle with bread crumbs, dot with butter; bake at 350°F (180°C) for about 20 minutes.
5. Remove from oven, sprinkle with cheese, bake until cheese is melted, about 10 minutes.

Serves 6-8

1 Serving (using 6 servings)

Energy — Calories	118	Cholesterol	1 mg
— kJ	495	Carbohydrate	11 g
Protein	10 g	Sodium	98 mg
Total Fat	5 g		

Eggplant is a member of the potato family. It is actually a fruit that is cooked as a vegetable.

Spicy Garden Stir-Fry

This stir-fry is very versatile and colourful. Use any combination of your favourite vegetables.

6 cups	assorted vegetables,
	  broccoli, sliced stems
	   and florets,
	  cauliflower, florets
	  carrots, thinly sliced
	  asparagus, 2" (5 cm) lengths
	  snowpeas
	  celery, diagonally sliced
	  onions, cut in small wedges
	  red, yellow and green peppers,
	   seeded, cut in strips
	  green onions, diagonally sliced
	  mushrooms, sliced
	  cherry tomatoes, halved
	  cabbage, spinach or bok choy,
	   shredded
		1.5 L

STIR-FRY SAUCE:

1 tbsp.	cornstarch	15 mL
1 tbsp.	water	15 mL
½ cup	vegetable stock	125 mL
¼ cup	dry sherry	60 mL
2 tbsp.	soy sauce	30 mL
1 tbsp.	Chinese chili sauce* or oyster sauce	15 mL
2 tsp.	sesame oil	10 mL
½ tsp.	sugar	2 mL
2 tbsp.	vegetable oil	30 mL
3	garlic cloves, minced	3
1 tbsp.	minced fresh ginger (optional) salt and pepper to taste	15 mL

Spicy Garden Stir-Fry

(Continued)

1. Prepare 6 cups (1.5 L) of vegetables of your choice. Keep broccoli, cauliflower and carrots together.
2. To make sauce, combine the next 8 ingredients in a small bowl.
3. Heat a wok over very high heat. Add oil. Add garlic and ginger and stir-fry for a few seconds. Add broccoli, cauliflower and carrots, if using. Stir-fry for 2-3 minutes.
4. Add remaining vegetables and stir-fry until colours intensify, about 2-3 minutes.
5. Pour Stir-Fry Sauce over vegetables. Lower heat; stir and cook until sauce thickens and glazes vegetables, about 2 minutes. Add salt and pepper to taste. Serve hot with rice.

Serves 4

* Use Chili Sauce for spicier flavour; use Oyster Sauce for milder flavour.

Variation: *Serve Spicy Garden Stir-Fry over linguine, fettuccine or your favourite Oriental noodles. You may want to double the sauce recipe if you are serving it over noodles.*

1 Serving (sauce only as vegetables vary)

Energy — **Calories**	**123**	**Cholesterol**	**0 mg**
— **kJ**	**516**	**Carbohydrate**	**6 g**
Protein	**1 g**	**Sodium**	**510 mg**
Total Fat	**9 g**		

Broccoli is a member of the cabbage family. It is high in fibre and a good source of vitamins C and A, plus riboflavin, calcium and iron.

Vegetarian Stir-Fry

These crisp colourful vegetables appeal to the eye and the taste buds.

1 lb.	tofu, cubed	500 g
2 tbsp.	soy sauce	30 mL
1 tsp.	ground ginger	5 mL
1 tbsp.	vegetable oil	15 mL
1	medium onion, thinly sliced	1
2	garlic cloves, minced	2
2	celery stalks, sliced	2
2	broccoli stalks, peeled and sliced	2
2	medium carrots, diced	2
	salt and pepper to taste	

1. In a bowl combine tofu with soy sauce and ginger.
2. Heat oil in a wok, stir-fry onions and garlic until soft and translucent.
3. Add celery, broccoli, carrots, marinated tofu, salt and pepper. Stir until vegetables are tender, but crisp. Serve over hot rice.

Serves 4

See photograph on front cover.

1 Serving

Energy	— Calories	146	Cholesterol	0 mg
	— kJ	609	Carbohydrate	13 g
Protein		10 g	Sodium	553 mg
Total Fat		7 g		

Tofu, also known as soya bean curd, is one of the world's most popular sources of high-quality, low-cost protein. It is cholesterol-free. Tofu can be substituted for cottage cheese in any recipe. Try it in lasagne.

Curried Soya Cubes

This dish has a "meaty" flavour and texture.

1½ cups	water	375 mL
¼ lb.	Betty K soya cubes	125 g
2 tbsp.	vegetable oil	30 mL
1	onion, sliced	1
2	garlic cloves, minced	2
1 tbsp.	curry powder	15 mL
1 tsp.	ground cumin	5 mL
1 tsp.	chili powder	5 mL
½ tsp.	paprika	2 mL
	salt and pepper to taste	
2 tsp.	lime juice	10 mL

1. In a small saucepan, heat water, add soya cubes; cook until water is absorbed. Remove from heat; set aside.
2. Heat oil, sauté onion and garlic until soft; add curry powder and soya cubes, cook for about 3 minutes.
3. Add cumin, chili powder, paprika, salt and pepper; cook, covered, over low heat for about 15 minutes. Add lime juice, stir and remove from heat. Serve with rice and salad.

Serves 4

1 Serving

Energy	**— Calories**	184	**Cholesterol**	0 mg
	— kJ	770	**Carbohydrate**	13 g
Protein		12 g	**Sodium**	8 mg
Total Fat		11 g		

Soya cubes are a textured protein made from soya bean flour.

Sweet and Sour Tofu with Peppers

This satisfying dish has a wonderful sweet and sour sauce.

1	green bell pepper	1
1	red bell pepper	1
2 tbsp.	vegetable oil	30 mL
19 oz.	can pineapple chunks	540 mL
1 tbsp.	cornstarch	15 mL
1/4 cup	soy sauce	60 mL
1/4 cup	honey	60 mL
1/4 cup	ketchup	60 mL
3 tbsp.	vinegar	45 mL
1 tsp.	Chinese spice	5 mL
	salt and pepper to taste	
1	small onion, chopped	1
2 lbs.	tofu	1 kg

1. Cut peppers into 1/4" (1 cm) pieces, sauté in oil for about 5 minutes. Remove from heat.
2. Drain off pineapple juice and mix with cornstarch, soy sauce, honey, ketchup, vinegar, Chinese spice, salt and pepper, until smooth.
3. Heat the pineapple juice mixture until it bubbles and thickens, about 10-15 minutes.
4. Add onion, crumbled tofu, pineapple chunks and peppers. Cook, stirring for a few minutes. Serve with hot rice.

Serves 4-6

1 Serving (using 4 servings)

Energy	— Calories	382	Cholesterol	0 mg
	— kJ	1600	Carbohydrate	54 g
Protein		17 g	Sodium	1207 mg
Total Fat		15 g		

Tofu Burgers

Tofu is unique in that it is low in calories and low in saturated fats. Its mildly nutty flavour is enhanced by spices and sauces which it readily absorbs.

2 lbs.	tofu	1 kg
2 cups	fine bread crumbs	500 mL
1 tbsp.	soy sauce	15 mL
1 tsp.	garlic powder	5 mL
1/2 cup	chopped celery	125 mL
	salt and pepper to taste	
1	small onion, finely chopped	1
	vegetable oil for frying	

1. In a bowl, mash tofu with a fork. Add bread crumbs, soy sauce, garlic powder, celery, salt, pepper and onion. Mix well.
2. Form into 3" (7 cm) patties. Pan-fry in a nonstick pan in oil until golden brown. Serve hot on a bun.

Serves 4-6

1 Serving (using 4 servings)

Energy — Calories	355	Cholesterol	3 mg
— kJ	1484	Carbohydrate	48 g
Protein	21 g	Sodium	682 mg
Total Fat	10 g		

Soya beans have been used in China for over 4,000 years. Unlike other legumes they are low in carbohydrates. High in protein, soya beans are rich in most minerals and vitamins, although they have only a moderate amount of vitamin A. Soya beans are used to produce many products: tofu, soya bean oil, soya flour, soy milk, soy sauce, miso, tempeh, tamari and sprouts. The iron in soya beans can be readily assimilated.

Chickpea Burgers

These burgers have great flavour and texture.

1	egg	1
2 tbsp.	chopped parsley	30 mL
1 tsp.	ground cumin	5 mL
1 tsp.	chili powder	5 mL
2 tbsp.	light butter	30 mL
2	garlic cloves, minced	2
1	small onion, finely chopped	1
1/4 cup	low-fat cottage cheese	60 mL
1 cup	cooked chickpeas	250 mL
1/4 cup	Betty K soya mince	60 mL
2 tbsp.	vegetable oil	30 mL

1. In a blender, combine egg, parsley, cumin, chili powder and butter. Blend until smooth.
2. Add garlic, onion, cottage cheese and chickpeas. Process in blender at low speed.
3. Stir in soya mince and let mixture stand for 10-15 minutes for soya mince to absorb moisture from other ingredients. Form mixture into 4 patties.
4. Pan-fry in a nonstick pan in hot oil until golden brown on both sides.

Serves 4

Variation: *Use tofu instead of cottage cheese.*

1 Serving

Energy — Calories	153	Cholesterol	72 mg
— kJ	640	Carbohydrate	15 g
Protein	10 g	Sodium	129 mg
Total Fat	6 g		

Also called garbanzo beans and ceci, chickpeas are usually a pale golden colour, but they can be white, yellow, red or black. Like other legumes, they are high in protein.

76

Tomato Bean Chili

Try this with the toppings. They add fresh flavour and colour.

2 tbsp.	oil	30 mL
4	garlic cloves, minced	4
2 cups	chopped onion	500 mL
3 cups	sliced fresh mushrooms	750 mL
2	red or green peppers, diced	2
3	celery stalks, finely chopped	3
2x28 oz.	can tomatoes	2x796 mL
28 oz.	can kidney beans	796 mL
28 oz.	can chickpeas	796 mL
2-3 tbsp.	chili powder	30-45 mL
2 tsp.	ground cumin	10 mL
1 tbsp.	oregano	15 mL
2 tsp.	basil	10 mL
1 tsp.	crushed red pepper	5 mL
1 tsp.	black pepper	5 mL
1 tsp.	salt	5 mL
2 tbsp.	chopped parsley	30 mL
	cooked rice.	

1. In a large saucepan, heat oil and sauté garlic, onions and mushrooms, until onions are translucent. Add peppers and celery and sauté for 3 minutes.
2. Add remaining ingredients and bring to a boil. Lower heat and simmer for 1-1$^{1}/_{2}$ hours.
3. Serve hot in flat soup plates with cooked white or brown rice.

Serves 10

Variation: *Top with chopped tomato, onion, red or green peppers, sour cream and grated Cheddar cheese.*

1 Serving

Energy — Calories	213	Cholesterol	3 mg
— kJ	891	Carbohydrate	35 g
Protein	10 g	Sodium	445 mg
Total Fat	5 g		

Vegetable Samosas

These triangular vegetable-filled patties are spicy and incredibly good.

PASTRY:

3 cups	flour	750 mL
	salt to taste	
4 tbsp.	oil	60 mL
	water	

FILLING:

2 lbs.	potatoes	1 kg
2 tbsp.	oil	30 mL
1	small onion, finely chopped	1
1 lb.	frozen peas	500 g
1/2 tsp.	garlic powder	2 mL
1/2 tsp.	cumin	2 mL
1 tsp.	chili powder	5 mL
1 tsp.	paprika	5 mL
	salt and pepper to taste	
1/2 tsp.	garam masala	2 mL
1 tbsp.	lemon juice	15 mL
	oil for frying	

1. Mix flour, salt, oil and enough water to make a pliable dough. Knead well. Let stand for 1 hour.
2. Boil potatoes until tender, drain and cool. Cut into very small cubes.
3. Heat oil, sauté onion until translucent. Stir in frozen peas, garlic powder, cumin, chili powder, paprika, salt and pepper. Cook, covered, for about 10 minutes.
4. Add diced potatoes, garam masala and lemon juice. Cook until dry.

Vegetable Samosas

(Continued)

TO SHAPE SAMOSAS:

1. Make a flour and water paste (equal portions of flour and water) to glue samosas together.
2. Divide the rested dough into balls 1½" (4 cm) in diameter. Roll dough out into circles of 4" (10 cm) in diameter. Brush each circle with oil on 1 side, sprinkle with flour and join 2 circles together. Roll these double circles to circles 8" (20 cm) in diameter. Place in a dry nonstick frying pan over medium heat, cook for 1 minute, turn and repeat.
3. While still hot cut the circles in half, separate halves. Each circle makes 2 cones. Place each half (a) on a working surface, (b) fold over ⅓. Brush the top ⅓ with flour and water paste; (c) fold the remaining ⅓ over and (d) you now have a cone.

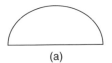

| (a) | (b) | (c) | (d) |

4. Put the filling mixture into the cone, fold the top over and seal with flour-water paste. Ensure the whole samosa is very well sealed or it will burst while cooking.
5. In hot oil (365°F [180°C]), deep-fry samosas for about 15 minutes. Drain on paper towels, let rest for 10 minutes.
6. Grill slowly under a broiler until golden brown. Serve hot

Makes about 30

1 Samosa (oil for frying not included)

Energy	— Calories	123	Cholesterol	0 mg
	— kJ	514	Carbohydrate	21 g
Protein		3 g	Sodium	11 mg
Total Fat		3 g		

Chili Bean Taco

A touch of Mexico, tacos are very tasty Mexican versions of the sandwich.

8	taco shells	8
1	small onion, chopped	1
1	garlic clove, minced	1
2 tsp.	light butter	10 mL
2 cups	cooked red kidney beans	500 mL
1 tbsp.	chili powder	15 mL
1 tsp.	ground cumin	5 mL
½ cup	grated low-fat Cheddar cheese	125 mL
1 cup	hot taco sauce	250 mL
1 cup	shredded lettuce	250 mL
1 cup	shredded carrots	250 mL

1. In a 350°F (180°C) oven, heat taco shells for 5-10 minutes.
2. Sauté onion and garlic in butter until soft, add kidney beans, chili powder and cumin. Stir and mash the beans while cooking. Remove from heat after beans are mashed and hot.
3. To assemble tacos — place 2-3 tbsp. (30-45 mL) of beans across the bottom of each taco shell, sprinkle with cheese then with sauce. Top with shredded lettuce and carrots and serve.

Serves 4

1 Serving (2 tacos)

Energy	— Calories	289	Cholesterol	8 mg
	— kJ	1208	Carbohydrate	51 g
Protein		13 g	Sodium	477 mg
Total Fat		5 g		

Chili powder is a mixture of powdered, dried chili peppers, garlic, oregano, cloves, cumin and coriander.

Macaroni and Baked Beans

Pasta spiced with cumin for a rich, appetizing flavour.

1¹/₂ cups	uncooked macaroni	375 mL
1	onion, finely chopped	1
2 tbsp.	vegetable oil	30 mL
1	green pepper, sliced in rings	1
1	tomato, diced	1
1 tsp.	cumin powder	5 mL
¹/₂ tsp.	turmeric	2 mL
	salt and pepper to taste	
19 oz.	can baked beans in tomato sauce	540 mL
¹/₂ cup	grated low-fat Cheddar cheese	125 mL

1. In a large saucepan, bring 2 quarts (2 L) of water to a boil; add macaroni and boil until tender, about 15 minutes. Drain, rinse in cold water, set aside in colander.
2. Sauté onion in oil, add pepper rings, tomato, cumin, turmeric, salt and pepper, cook for 2 minutes. Add baked beans and mix well.
3. In a casserole, arrange ¹/₂ of the macaroni, ¹/₂ of the bean curry, then add a layer of macaroni and cover with the rest of the beans.
4. Bake at 350°F (180°C) for 10 minutes. Remove from oven, sprinkle with grated cheese and bake until cheese is melted, about 5 minutes.

Serves 6

1 Serving

Energy	— Calories	377	Cholesterol	10 mg
	— kJ	1578	Carbohydrate	55 g
Protein		16 g	Sodium	838 mg
Total Fat		10 g		

Curried Okra and Macaroni

Okra is also known as "ladies fingers" in some countries.

1	large onion, cubed	1
1	hot pepper, seeded	1
2	garlic cloves, halved	2
2 tbsp.	curry powder	30 mL
2	large tomatoes, quartered	2
1 lb.	okra	500 g
3 tbsp.	vegetable oil	45 mL
2	potatoes, quartered	2
½ cup	macaroni	125 mL
2 cups	water	500 mL
	salt and pepper to taste	

1. Blend onion, pepper, garlic, curry powder and tomatoes into a paste.
2. Cut okra into 1" (2.5 cm) pieces, set aside.
3. Heat oil, add curry mixture. Stir-fry for 2 minutes.
4. Add okra, potato and macaroni, stir; add water and bring to a boil. Simmer, covered, until potatoes and macaroni are tender. Add salt and pepper to taste. Serve immediately.

Serves 6-8

1 Serving (using 6 servings)

Energy	— Calories	163	Cholesterol	0 mg
	— kJ	682	Carbohydrate	22 g
Protein		4 g	Sodium	82 mg
Total Fat		8 g		

Okra is native to tropical Africa. It is a fair source of vitamins A and C. Used for both its flavour and thickening properties, it is used in soups and stews, especially well-known in Creole Gumbo. Add sliced raw okra to salads. It is very good with tomatoes.

Meatless Spaghetti Sauce

Soya mince gives this inexpensive but nutritious sauce a "meaty" texture.

1	medium onion, chopped	1
2	garlic cloves, minced	2
2 tbsp.	vegetable oil	30 mL
1	eggplant, peeled and cut into ½" (1.3 cm) pieces	1
½ lb.	mushrooms, sliced	250 g
¼ cup	Betty K soya mince	60 mL
½ tsp.	paprika	2 mL
¼ tsp.	hot pepper flakes salt and pepper to taste	1 mL
28 oz.	can tomatoes	796 mL
1 lb.	spaghetti	500 g
2 tbsp.	chopped parsley	30 mL
½ cup	grated Parmesan cheese	125 mL

1. Sauté onion and garlic in oil until translucent; add eggplant, cook about 10 minutes.
2. Stir in mushrooms, soya mince, paprika, hot pepper flakes, salt and pepper.
3. Add tomatoes with juice, bring to a boil, cook, uncovered, on medium heat until sauce is thick, about 25 minutes.
4. Cook spaghetti in a large pot of boiling salted water until just tender, about 8-10 minutes. Drain well.
5. Toss spaghetti with sauce, parsley and cheese.

Serves 4-6

1 Serving (using 4 servings)

Energy — Calories	638	Cholesterol	8 mg
— kJ	2669	Carbohydrate	107 g
Protein	24 g	Sodium	465 mg
Total Fat	12 g		

Fresh Garden Pasta

This pasta dish has wonderful colour & texture.

1 lb.	fusilli, fettuccine or spaghetti	500 g
2 tbsp.	oil	30 mL
2	garlic cloves, minced	2
2	large ripe tomatoes, chopped	2
2	small zucchini, thinly sliced	2
1	each, sweet red and green pepper, seeded, thinly sliced	1
6	green onions, diagonally sliced	6
2	celery stalks, diagonally sliced	2
1 cup	broccoli florets	250 mL
1/2 lb.	snowpeas, trimmed	250 g
1/2 cup	chopped red onion	125 mL
1/2 cup	chopped fresh mixed herbs (parsley, basil, oregano, chives)	125 mL
1/4-1/2 lb.	skim-milk feta cheese	125-250 g
1 cup	Italian or Greek black olives grated Parmesan cheese	250 mL

1. In a large saucepan, bring 4-quarts (4 L) of salted water to a boil. Add pasta and cook until tender but firm, al dente, 3-4 minutes for fresh pasta, 10-15 minutes for dry.
2. In a large saucepan, heat oil and sauté garlic until golden. Add vegetables and herbs. If you want fresh crunchy vegetables, add feta cheese, olives and hot pasta immediately. Turn off heat. The hot pasta will warm the vegetables and slightly melt the cheese. For less crunchy vegetables, stir-fry vegetables and herbs with the oil and garlic for 3-5 minutes. Serve at once with Parmesan cheese.

Serves 6

See photograph opposite.

1 Serving

Energy — Calories	480	Cholesterol	17 mg
— kJ	2010	Carbohydrate	72 g
Protein	17 g	Sodium	1138 mg
Total Fat	14 g		

Main Course

Fresh Garden Pasta, page 84
Zucchini Salad, page 55
Chapatti, page 95

Peppery Tomato Pasta

This very simple sauce has a superb intense flavour. Use fresh tomatoes when they are available.

2 tbsp.	oil	30 mL
4	garlic cloves, minced	4
1 tsp.	crushed red pepper	5 mL
1	small onion, finely chopped	1
28 oz.	can of tomatoes	796 mL
1/2 cup	chopped fresh mixed herbs (chives, basil, oregano, parsley)	125 mL
1/4 tsp.	cayenne pepper	1 mL
	salt and pepper to taste	
1	large red pepper, seeded, diced (optional)	1
1 lb.	small pasta shells, fusilli or spaghettini	500 g
4 tbsp.	grated Parmesan cheese	60 mL

1. In a large saucepan, heat oil and gently sauté garlic, peppers and onion, until onion is translucent.
2. Stir in liquid from tomatoes and purée or coarsely chop tomatoes. Add to the saucepan with the herbs, cayenne pepper, salt, pepper and red pepper, if using. Simmer sauce for 15-20 minutes.
3. Cook pasta as directed on the package.
4. Drain pasta and add hot pasta to tomato sauce. Toss to combine pasta and sauce and blend flavours.
5. Serve with Parmesan cheese.

Serves 4

1 Serving

Energy — Calories	549	Cholesterol	4 mg
— kJ	2296	Carbohydrate	96 g
Protein	18 g	Sodium	370 mg
Total Fat	10 g		

Spinach Lasagne

Serve this family favourite with your favourite salad.

TOMATO SAUCE:

1	onion, chopped	1
1	garlic clove, minced	1
1 tbsp.	vegetable oil	15 mL
4 oz.	mushrooms, sliced	125 g
	salt and pepper to taste	
1/2 tsp.	oregano	2 mL
1/2 tsp.	basil	2 mL
1 tsp.	sugar	5 mL
2x19 oz.	cans whole tomatoes	2x540 mL

CHEESE SAUCE:

1/4 cup	light butter	60 mL
1/3 cup	flour	75 mL
	salt and pepper to taste	
2 cups	1% milk	500 mL
1/2 cup	grated low-fat Cheddar cheese	125 mL
3 tbsp.	grated Parmesan cheese	45 mL

6	lasagne noodles	6
1/2 lb.	frozen spinach, thawed	250 g
1/2 cup	grated low-fat Cheddar cheese	125 mL
3 tbsp.	grated Parmesan cheese	45 mL

1. To make tomato sauce, sauté onion and garlic in oil until translucent.
2. Add mushrooms, salt, pepper, oregano, basil, sugar and tomatoes. Bring to a boil. Simmer, covered, for 45 minutes.
3. Continue cooking, uncovered, for 15 minutes until sauce is thick. Remove from heat.

Spinach Lasagne

(Continued)

4. To make cheese sauce, melt butter; add flour, salt and pepper. Blend until smooth.
5. Stir over heat for 1 minute, gradually stir in milk; stir until sauce boils and thickens.
6. Remove from heat, stir in grated cheeses.
7. Boil lasagne noodles until tender, about 15 minutes. Drain.
8. Place 3 lasagne noodles in a 7 x 11" (18 x 28 cm) ovenproof dish. Spread 1/2 of tomato sauce over pasta, then 1/2 of cheese sauce.
9. Remove as much liquid as possible from thawed spinach; place spinach over cheese sauce.
10. Top with 3 lasagne noodles. Spread with remaining tomato sauce and cheese sauce. Sprinkle with Cheddar cheese then Parmesan cheese.
11. Bake at 350°F (180°C) for 40 minutes. Remove from oven, let stand for 10 minutes before serving.

Serves 6

1 Serving

Energy — **Calories**	**340**	**Cholesterol**	**41 mg**
— **kJ**	**1422**	**Carbohydrate**	**42 g**
Protein	**19 g**	**Sodium**	**896 mg**
Total Fat	**12 g**		

Spinach originated in the Middle East. It is rich in iron, vitamins A and C and has about 40% potassium. It is good for the urinary and digestive systems.

Vegetable Pullao Rice

This has a wonderful combination of flavours.

1	large onion, finely chopped	1
3	garlic cloves, minced	3
1	small piece fresh ginger, chopped	1
2 tbsp.	vegetable oil	30 mL
4	whole cloves	4
½ tsp.	chili powder	2 mL
1 tsp.	turmeric	5 mL
1 tsp.	garam masala	5 mL
½ cup	peas	125 mL
½ cup	corn kernels	125 mL
4	tomatoes, chopped	4
1	green pepper, chopped	1
2	hot peppers, chopped	2
2 cups	uncooked rice	500 mL
1	large potato, thinly sliced	1
	salt and pepper to taste	

1. Sauté onion, garlic and ginger in oil until soft. Add cloves, chili powder, turmeric and garam masala. Sauté for 1 minute.
2. Add peas, corn, tomatoes, green pepper and hot pepper. Simmer for 5 minutes.
3. Parboil rice in 4 cups (1 L) of water for about 10 minutes, leaving it slightly undercooked. Drain.
4. In a 9 x 13" (23 x 33 cm) ovenproof dish, layer pea and corn mixture, cover with uncooked potatoes, then with warm rice. Add salt and pepper.
5. Cover with foil and bake at 350°F (180°C) for about 1 hour.

Serves 4-6

1 Serving (using 4 servings)

Energy	— Calories	557	Cholesterol	0 mg
	— kJ	2828	Carbohydrate	110 g
Protein		12 g	Sodium	294 mg
Total Fat		8 g		

Rice Cook-Up

Coconut milk adds a subtle sweetness to this tropical rice dish.

1	large onion, chopped	1
2	garlic cloves, minced	2
1 tbsp.	vegetable oil	15 mL
1 tsp.	chopped fresh ginger	5 mL
1	carrot, diced	1
1	celery stalk, diced	1
1	green pepper, diced	1
1 cup	long-grain rice	250 mL
1 cup	coconut milk *	250 mL
1 cup	water	250 mL
19 oz.	can black-eye peas, drained **	540 mL
	salt and pepper to taste	
1/2 tsp.	hot pepper sauce	2 mL

1. Sauté onion and garlic in oil until soft; add ginger, carrot, celery and green pepper. Cook for 2 minutes.
2. Add rice, cook for 1 minute, add coconut milk and water, bring to a boil.
3. Add peas, salt, pepper and pepper sauce, reduce heat; simmer, covered, until liquid is absorbed, about 30 minutes.

Serves 4

* *See page 32*
** *Pigeon peas or chickpeas can be substituted*

1 Serving

Energy	— Calories	489	Cholesterol	0 mg
	— kJ	2287	Carbohydrate	68 g
Protein		13 g	Sodium	29 mg
Total Fat		19 g		

Vegetable Pizza

Adding tofu makes this pizza high protein.

½ cup	warm water	125 mL
1 tsp.	sugar	5 mL
1 tsp.	active dry yeast	5 mL
2 tsp.	vegetable oil	10 mL
1½ cups	flour	375 mL
¼ cup	grated low-fat mozzarella	60 mL

TOPPING:

1 cup	crumbled soft tofu	250 mL
1	onion, finely chopped	1
1	garlic clove, minced	1
1 tbsp.	vegetable oil	15 mL
4	tomatoes, diced	4
½ cup	sliced mushrooms	125 mL
1	green pepper, diced	1
1	zucchini, sliced	1
½ cup	chopped black olives	125 mL
1 tbsp.	oregano	15 mL
¼ cup	grated Parmesan cheese	60 mL
1 cup	grated low-fat mozzarella	250 mL

1. To make dough, combine water, sugar, yeast; let stand 5 minutes.
2. Add oil, stir in flour and cheese, mix. Form dough into a ball, set in a warm place for about 45 minutes.
3. To prepare topping, sauté first 10 topping ingredients. Cook for about 10 minutes. Remove from heat.
4. To make pizza, divide dough into 10 pieces. Roll out to 6" (15 cm) circles. Place on lightly oiled baking sheets. Cover crusts with topping. Sprinkle with cheeses. Bake at 375°F (190°C), 20-25 minutes.

Makes 10 pizzas

1 Pizza

Energy — Calories	190	Cholesterol	10 mg
— kJ	969	Carbohydrate	22 g
Protein	9 g	Sodium	353 mg
Total Fat	8 g		

Breads

"Pow"— Steamed Rolls

This Chinese roll is popular in the Caribbean.

PASTRY:

2 tsp.	active dry yeast	10 mL
1 tbsp.	sugar	15 mL
3 cups	flour	750 mL
1 tsp.	baking powder	5 mL
1 tsp.	salt	5 mL

FILLING:

1 lb.	potatoes	500 g
2 tbsp.	oil	30 mL
1	onion, diced	1
2	garlic cloves, minced	2
½ cup	sliced string beans	125 mL
½ cup	diced carrots	125 mL
¼ cup	chopped green onions	60 mL
	salt and pepper to taste	
1 tsp.	Chinese spice	5 mL
1 tbsp.	soy sauce	15 mL
1 tsp.	hot pepper sauce	5 mL

1. To make pastry, mix yeast and sugar in warm water — let stand until yeast rises, about 10 minutes.
2. Combine flour, baking powder and salt; add yeast and mix well to form a soft dough. Cover and leave to double in bulk, about 45 minutes.
3. Divide dough into small balls, about the size of a golf ball.
4. To make filling, peel potatoes, boil and cut into cubes.
5. Heat oil, sauté onion and garlic until soft. Add string beans and carrots — cook for about 10 minutes. Add potatoes, green onions, salt, pepper, Chinese spice, soy sauce and hot pepper sauce. Stir-fry for 5 minutes.
6. To assemble "POW", roll each ball of dough into a 4" (10 cm) circle.
7. Fill centre of each circle with 1-2 tbsp. (15-30 mL) of vegetable filling, shape dough around filling to form a ball.

"POW" — Steamed Roll

(Continued)

8. In a steamer, over boiling water, put each ball seam side down, on a piece of waxed paper, and steam for about 10 minutes. Cook about 4-5 rolls at a time, depending on the size of your steamer.

Makes about 12

1 Roll

Energy	**— Calories**	233	**Cholesterol**	0 mg
	— kJ	975	**Carbohydrate**	45 g
Protein		6 g	**Sodium**	292 mg
Total Fat		3 g		

Chapatti

This is an unleavened Indian whole-meal bread.

2 cups	whole-wheat flour	500 mL
1/2 tsp.	salt	2 mL
1 cup	water	250 mL
	light butter	

1. Mix flour and salt with just enough water to make a firm dough. Knead well. Place in a greased bowl and cover for about 1 hour.
2. Divide dough into 8 balls. Roll out each ball on a floured board to form a circle about 6" (15 cm) in diameter.
3. Cook dough circles on a heated, lightly greased griddle or tawa until bubbles form on upper side, turn and cook other side. Pat cooked chapatti with a little butter, if you wish.

Serves 4

See photograph on page 85.

1 Serving (2 chapatti)

Energy	**— Calories**	200	**Cholesterol**	0 mg
	— kJ	836	**Carbohydrate**	43 g
Protein		8 g	**Sodium**	240 mg
Total Fat		1 g		

"Sada" Roti

This savoury, onion and pepper roti is popular in Guyana among the Indian community.

2 cups	flour	500 mL
1 tsp.	baking powder	5 mL
1/4 tsp.	salt	1 mL
1	small onion, finely chopped	1
1/4 cup	chopped green onions	60 mL
1	small hot pepper, chopped	1
1 cup	water	250 mL

1. Mix flour, baking powder, salt, onion, green onions, and hot pepper with just enough water to make a firm dough. Cover with a damp towel and let dough rest for about 1 hour.
2. Divide dough into 6 balls, roll out each ball to about 5" (13 cm) in diameter.
3. Brown dough circles on each side, on heated lightly greased griddle or tawa, then place under the broiler until roti puffs up. Serve hot.

Makes 6

See photograph on front cover.

1 Serving

Energy	— Calories	172	Cholesterol	0 mg
	— kJ	721	Carbohydrate	36 g
Protein		5 g	Sodium	235 mg
Total Fat		0.5 g		

Chili peppers are native to tropical America. They are now important in Asian, African, South and North American cuisines. There are more than 200 varieties of these peppers and they vary from mild to fiery. They come in colours ranging from red and green to yellow to black and the lengths vary from 1/4" (1 cm) to 12" (30 cm).

Whole-Wheat Bread

This whole-grain bread is very satisfying.

5 cups	whole-wheat flour	1.25 L
3 tbsp.	brown sugar	45 mL
1 tsp.	salt	5 mL
3 tbsp.	light margarine	45 mL
2 tbsp.	active dry yeast	30 mL
1 cup	warm water	250 mL
1½ cups	lukewarm 1% milk	375 mL

1. Combine 4 cups (1 L) of flour, sugar, salt and margarine.
2. Dissolve yeast in lukewarm water, let stand for about 10 minutes, add warm milk. Add enough of this to flour mixture to make a soft dough.
3. Turn dough onto a lightly floured surface, knead in enough additional flour to make a stiff dough. Shape dough into a ball and place in a greased bowl.
4. Cover and let rise in a warm place until it doubles in bulk, about an hour.
5. Punch down, divide dough into 2 balls. Shape into 2 loaves and place in greased 5 x 9" (13 x 23 cm) pans. Let rise for another 45 minutes.
6. Bake at 375°F (190°C) for about 50 minutes, until brown and loaf begins to shrink from pan.

Makes 2 loaves

1 loaf

Energy	— Calories	1212	**Cholesterol**	7 mg
	— kJ	5073	**Carbohydrate**	242 g
Protein		48 g	**Sodium**	1204 mg
Total Fat		14 g		

Whole-wheat flour has a richer flavour than white flour. It also has more fibre and a higher nutritional and fat content. It retains the wheat germ and should be refrigerated to help prevent it from going rancid.

Pita Bread

This Middle Eastern bread is very versatile.

2 tsp.	active dry yeast	10 mL
2½ cups	lukewarm water	625 mL
8 cups	flour	2 L
1 tsp.	salt	5 mL
3 tbsp.	light vegetable oil	45 mL

1. Add yeast to 3 tbsp. (45 mL) of water — let stand for 5 minutes; stir in rest of water, leave for another 5 minutes.
2. Mix together flour, salt and vegetable oil; make a well in the flour mixture, pour in yeast. Mix and knead for about 20 minutes, until dough is elastic. Place dough in a lightly greased bowl, leave in a warm place for 40-50 minutes.
3. Punch down dough, divide it into 16 balls. Cover for 30 minutes.
4. Roll out each ball to about ¼" (1 cm) thick and bake on ungreased baking pans at 375°F (190°C) for about 10-15 minutes. Wrap pitas in foil and keep warm if serving immediately.

Makes 16 pitas

See photograph on page 17.

1 Pita

Energy	— Calories	273	Cholesterol	0 mg
	— kJ	1326	Carbohydrate	52 g
Protein		7 g	Sodium	121 mg
Total Fat		3 g		

Cornmeal Muffins

1 cup	cornmeal	250 mL
¾ cup	flour	175 mL
¼ tsp.	baking soda	1 mL
2 tsp.	baking powder	10 mL
2 tbsp.	sugar	30 mL
½ tsp.	salt	2 mL
1	egg, beaten	1
3 tbsp.	melted butter	45 mL
1 cup	buttermilk	250 mL

Cornmeal Muffins

(Continued)

1. Combine all the dry ingredients.
2. Add beaten egg, melted butter and buttermilk, blend lightly.
3. Bake in greased muffin pans at 400°F (200°C), for 15-20 minutes.

Makes 12, 2¹/₂" (6 cm) muffins

See photograph on page 51.

1 Muffin

Energy	— Calories	127	Cholesterol	32 mg
	— kJ	533	Carbohydrate	20 g
Protein		3 g	Sodium	231 mg
Total Fat		4 g		

Oatmeal Date Muffins

2 cups	whole-wheat flour	500 mL
2 cups	rolled oats	500 mL
3 tsp.	baking powder	15 mL
1¹/₂ tsp.	baking soda	7 mL
1 tsp.	allspice	5 mL
²/₃ cup	finely chopped dates	150 mL
2	eggs, beaten	2
2 cups	1% milk	500 mL
¹/₄ cup	canola oil	60 mL
¹/₃ cup	honey	75 mL

1. In a large bowl, combine dry ingredients. Add dates, mixing well.
2. To the beaten eggs add milk, oil and honey. Stir into flour mixture.
3. Pour batter into nonstick medium-sized muffin pans. Bake at 375°F (190°C) for 15-20 minutes.

Makes 24 muffins

1 Muffin

Energy	— Calories	125	Cholesterol	24 mg
	— kJ	523	Carbohydrate	21 g
Protein		4 g	Sodium	152 mg
Total Fat		4 g		

Zucchini Bread

This bread is moist and flavourful with a touch of lemon.

2 cups	flour	500 mL
1 cup	sugar	250 mL
3/4 cup	chopped walnuts	175 mL
1 tbsp.	baking powder	15 mL
1/2 tsp.	salt	2 mL
3	eggs	3
1/2 cup	canola oil	125 mL
1 1/2 cups	grated zucchini	375 mL
1 tsp.	grated lemon rind	5 mL

1. Combine flour, sugar, nuts, baking powder and salt.
2. Beat eggs, stir in oil, zucchini and lemon rind. Add flour mixture and combine.
3. Pour batter into 2, 5 x 9" (13 x 23 cm) greased loaf pans. Bake at 350°F (180°C) for 1 hour. Cool in pans for 10 minutes, then remove.

Makes 2 loaves, 15 slices per loaf

1 Slice

Energy	— Calories	252	Cholesterol	55 mg
	— kJ	1053	Carbohydrate	32 g
Protein		4 g	Sodium	187 mg
Total Fat		12 g		

A member of the squash family, zucchinis range in colour from dark to light green to yellow. They are a good source of potassium, vitamins A and C and niacin.

Banana Bread

Nutmeg enhances the rich banana flavour of this lovely bread.

2 cups	flour	500 mL
1 tbsp.	baking powder	15 mL
1/2 tsp.	salt	2 mL
1/2 tsp.	nutmeg	2 mL
1/2 cup	light butter	125 mL
1 cup	sugar	250 mL
1	egg, beaten	1
3	ripe bananas, mashed	3
1/2 cup	milk	125 mL
1 tsp.	vanilla	5 mL

1. Sift together flour, baking powder, salt and nutmeg.
2. Cream butter and sugar until light, add beaten egg and mashed bananas. Mix well.
3. Add flour gradually to creamed mixture, alternating with milk and vanilla. Mixture should be thick. Pour into a greased 5 x 9" (13 x 23 cm) loaf pan.
4. Bake at 350°F (180°C) for 1 hour. Bread is done when a skewer inserted in the centre comes out clean.

Makes 1 loaf

1 Loaf

Energy	— Calories	3365	Cholesterol	541 mg
	— kJ	14081	Carbohydrate	566 g
Protein		45 g	Sodium	3691 mg
Total Fat		109 g		

Bananas have been grown in India for over 4,000 years and are now cultivated in most tropical countries. They are easily digested and are high in vitamin C, potassium and carbohydrates. Bananas are low in fats and protein.

Coconut Bread

This delicious bread is popular in the Caribbean Islands.

4 cups	flour	1 L
2 tsp.	baking powder	10 mL
1/2 tsp.	salt	2 mL
2 cups	grated fresh coconut (or desiccated)	500 mL
3/4 cup	sugar	175 mL
1 tsp.	vanilla	5 mL
1	egg, beaten	1
1 cup	1% milk	250 mL
	sugar	

1. Sift together flour, baking powder and salt. Add coconut, sugar, vanilla and egg. Mix well.
2. Add milk a little at a time until dough is firm but not sticky.
3. Knead for a few minutes. Shape dough into 2 loaves and place into greased 5 x 9" (13 x 23 cm) loaf pans.
4. Dust dough with sugar and bake at 350°F (180°C) for 1 hour, or until golden brown.

Makes 2 loaves

1 Loaf

Energy	— Calories	2042	Cholesterol	142 mg
	— kJ	8544	Carbohydrate	328 g
Protein		42 g	Sodium	1096 mg
Total Fat		65 g		

Coconuts originated in Malaysia. If buying fresh coconuts choose one with liquid. Coconuts are very high in fat, but coconut milk compares to mother's milk in chemical balance. In its natural state it is quite a complete protein food. See page 32 for Coconut milk.

Dessert

Desserts

Sweet Potato Pone

This is popular in Trinidad.

1 cup	grated cassava	250 mL
2 cups	grated sweet potato	500 mL
½ cup	grated pumpkin	125 mL
½ cup	light margarine or butter	125 mL
1 cup	sugar	250 mL
½ tsp.	allspice	2 mL
¼ tsp.	white pepper	1 mL
2 tsp.	vanilla essence (extract)	10 mL
1 cup	coconut milk*	250 mL

1. Mix cassava, sweet potato and pumpkin with margarine.
2. Add sugar, allspice, pepper and vanilla essence. Blend well, adding enough coconut milk to bind mixture.
3. Bake in a shallow, greased 8" (20 cm) square casserole at 350°F (180°C) for about 1 hour, until top is brown and firm. Cool and cut into squares.

* See page 32.

Serves 10

1 Serving (using margarine for analysis)

Energy	— Calories	300	Cholesterol	0 mg
	— kJ	1255	Carbohydrate	40 g
Protein		2 g	Sodium	137 mg
Total Fat		16 g		

Sweet potatoes are native to tropical America. There are two types: one is mealy when cooked and the other is darker, sweeter and more moist. These are sometimes, incorrectly, called yams. Sweet potatoes are high in vitamins A and C and a good source of niacin.

Ruth's Carrot Cake

This delicious recipe was given to me by a good friend in Melfort, Saskatchewan.

2 cups	flour	500 mL
2 tsp.	baking powder	10 mL
1½ tsp.	baking soda	7 mL
1 tsp.	salt	5 mL
2 tsp.	cinnamon	10 mL
2 cups	white sugar	500 mL
1½ cups	vegetable oil	375 mL
4	eggs	4
2 cups	finely grated carrots	500 mL
19 oz.	can drained, crushed pineapple	540 mL
½ cup	finely chopped walnuts or pecans	125 mL
1 cup	finely grated coconut	250 mL
1 cup	chopped raisins (optional)	250 mL

1. In a large bowl, combine flour, baking powder, baking soda, salt, cinnamon and sugar. Add oil and eggs, mixing well.
2. Blend in carrots, pineapple, walnuts, coconut and raisins.
3. Place batter in a greased 9 x 13" (23 x 33 cm) pan. Bake at 350°F (180°C) for about ¾ hour.

CREAM CHEESE ICING:

8 oz.	light cream cheese	250 g
½ cup	light margarine or butter	125 mL
2 tsp.	vanilla essence (extract)	10 mL
1 cup	sifted icing sugar	250 mL

1. Beat together the first 3 ingredients and add enough sugar to give icing a good spreading consistency.

Serves 18

1 Serving

Energy — Calories	497	Cholesterol	67 mg
— kJ	2080	Carbohydrate	55 g
Protein	6 g	Sodium	459 mg
Total Fat	30 g		

Zucchini Cake

A delicious cake for both vegetarians and non-vegetarians.

4	medium-sized zucchini	4
3/4 cup	chopped walnuts	175 mL
2 cups	flour	500 mL
1 1/2 tsp.	baking powder	7 mL
3/4 tsp.	baking soda	3 mL
1 tsp.	allspice	5 mL
1 tsp.	salt	5 mL
4	eggs	4
2 cups	sugar	500 mL
2/3 cup	vegetable oil	150 mL
1 tsp.	vanilla essence (extract)	5 mL
1 cup	1% milk	250 mL
1 tbsp.	lemon juice	15 mL

1. Grate unpeeled zucchini. Measure 3 cups (750 mL), press out as much liquid as possible; zucchini should now measure 2 cups (500 mL). Mix in nuts.
2. In a large bowl, combine flour, baking powder, baking soda, allspice and salt. Set aside.
3. In a large bowl, beat eggs, sugar and oil at high speed until light. Stir in vanilla.
4. Mix milk and lemon juice together. Beat the flour mixture alternately with milk mixture into the egg mixture.
5. Add zucchini and nuts, stirring until evenly distributed.
6. Bake in a 9 x 13" (23 x 33 cm) pan at 350°F (180°C) for 40-45 minutes. Leave in pan to cool before serving.

Serves 18

1 Serving

Energy — Calories	295	Cholesterol	61 mg
— kJ	1236	Carbohydrate	42 g
Protein	5 g	Sodium	220 mg
Total Fat	13 g		

Cecil's Cheesecake

This is my husband's favourite cheesecake.

1 cup	graham wafer crumbs	250 mL
1/4 cup	light butter	60 mL
1 cup	sugar	250 mL
3x8 oz.	pkgs. light cream cheese	3x250 g
4	eggs, beaten	4
2 tsp.	vanilla essence (extract)	10 mL
2 cups	light sour cream	500 mL
	food colouring (optional)	

1. To make the crust, combine wafer crumbs with melted butter and 1 tbsp. (15 mL) of sugar.
2. Spread over bottom of 10" (25 cm) springform pan and bake for 8 minutes at 350°F (180°C).
3. To make the filling, blend cream cheese, add eggs, 1 tsp. (5 mL) of vanilla and 3/4 cup (175 mL) of sugar, mixing well.
4. Pour filling over graham wafer crust and bake at 375°F (190°C) for 35 minutes.
5. To make the topping, mix sour cream with 1 tbsp. (15 mL) of sugar and 1 tsp. (5 mL) vanilla. Add a few drops of the food colour of your choice. Spread evenly over baked cheesecake. Bake at 375°F (190°C) for 5 minutes. Refrigerate, covered, overnight. Serve with seasonal fresh fruit if you wish.

Serves 12

See photograph on page 103.

1 Serving

Energy — Calories	360	Cholesterol	148 mg
— kJ	1507	Carbohydrate	31 g
Protein	10 g	Sodium	395 mg
Total Fat	22 g		

Raisin Cheese Pie

Cheddar and orange give added interest to this raisin pie.

FILLING:

½ cup	sugar	125 mL
4 tbsp.	cornstarch	60 mL
2 cups	raisins	500 mL
1½ cups	water	375 mL
¼ tsp.	salt	1 mL
1 tbsp.	light margarine	15 mL
1	orange, all rind of and half of juice	1
1 tbsp.	lemon juice	15 mL
1 cup	grated Cheddar cheese	250 mL

PASTRY:

2 cups	flour	500 mL
1 tsp.	salt	5 mL
⅔ cup	light margarine	150 mL
6 tbsp.	cold water	90 mL
	milk	

1. Combine sugar and cornstarch. Blend well. Add raisins and water, cook over medium heat until thick.
2. Remove from heat, add salt, margarine, orange rind, juice of half an orange and lemon juice. Mix well. Cool filling.
3. Stir together flour and salt, cut in margarine and blend until mixture resembles meal.
4. Add cold water, a little at a time, until mixture is moistened. Form dough into 2 balls.
5. On a lightly floured board roll 1 ball to 12" (22 cm) diameter. Transfer to a 9" (23 cm) pie plate, trim pastry to fit rim of pie plate.
6. For top crust, roll out second ball of dough.
7. Pour filling into uncooked pastry shell. Sprinkle cheese over filling.

Raisin Cheese Pie

(Continued)

8. Cover with pastry for top crust; trim off excess pastry and flute edges. Cut steam vents in pastry. Brush crust with a little milk.
9. Bake at 375°F (190°C) for 15-20 minutes.

Serves 6

1 Serving

Energy — Calories	608	Cholesterol	20 mg
— kJ	2544	Carbohydrate	102 g
Protein	11 g	Sodium	798 mg
Total Fat	19 g		

Bread and Butter Custard

1 tbsp.	light butter	15 mL
2-3	slices of bread	2-3
3	eggs	3
1 tsp.	vanilla essence (extract)	5 mL
½ tsp.	allspice	2 mL
1 cup	2% evaporated milk	250 mL
1 cup	1% milk	250 mL
1 tbsp.	sugar	15 mL

1. Butter bread, cut into small pieces and arrange in a shallow 8" (20 cm) square pyrex dish.
2. Beat eggs, add vanilla, allspice, evaporated milk and milk.
3. Pour custard over bread, let stand for ½ hour.
4. Sprinkle with sugar. Bake at 350°F (180°C) for 1 hour.

Serves 4-6

1 Serving (using 4 servings)

Energy — Calories	336	Cholesterol	211 mg
— kJ	1407	Carbohydrate	23 g
Protein	12 g	Sodium	218 mg
Total Fat	23 g		

Peach Cobbler

This old-fashioned dessert is a family treat.

¹/₂ cup	light butter	125 mL

BATTER:

³/₄ cup	flour	175 mL
1 cup	sugar	250 mL
2 tsp.	baking powder	10 mL
¹/₄ tsp.	salt	1 mL
³/₄ cup	1% milk	175 mL

TOPPING:

2 cups	sliced raw peaches	500 mL
1 cup	brown sugar	250 mL
1 tsp.	cinnamon	5 mL

1. Put butter in a 8" (20 cm) square pan in 350°F (180°C) oven for a few minutes, to melt.
2. Blend flour and sugar with baking powder, salt and milk to make a smooth batter.
3. Pour batter as evenly as possible over melted butter.
4. Combine peaches, sugar and cinnamon.
5. Arrange on top of batter. Bake at 350°F (180°C) for 1 hour.

Serves 6

1 Serving

Energy — Calories	533	Saturated Fat	10 g
— kJ	2231	Cholesterol	45 mg
Protein	3 g	Carbohydrate	96 g
Total Fat	17 g	Sodium	431 mg

Native to China, peaches are high in vitamin A and also contain vitamin C.

Banana Fritters

These are wonderful for a special breakfast or as a dessert.

1	egg	1
	pinch of salt	
1 tsp.	sugar	5 mL
1 tbsp.	flour	15 mL
⅔ cup	1%milk	150 mL
3	bananas	3
	oil for frying	
	castor sugar (granulated)	

1. Beat egg with salt and sugar. Fold in flour and milk to make a thin batter.
2. Slice bananas and add to batter.
3. Heat 1 tbsp. (15 mL) oil in a nonstick pan, add batter by the tablespoonful (15 mL) to make 3" (7 cm) fritters. Pan-fry until golden brown on both sides. Add more oil as needed. Drain fritters on paper towels, keep warm.
4. Sprinkle sugar lightly on top. Serve hot.

Serves 4-6

1 Serving (4 servings used — oil for frying not included)

Energy — Calories	151	Saturated Fat	1 g
— kJ	631	Cholesterol	70 mg
Protein	4 g	Carbohydrate	31 g
Total Fat	2 g	Sodium	84 mg

Bananas are one of the few fruits that develop a better flavour when they are ripened after being picked. To ripen green bananas, leave, uncovered, at room temperature. To speed up ripening, place bananas in a perforated paper bag.

Yogurt-Filled Melon

This is refreshing and nutritious.

2 cups	1% plain yogurt	500 mL
2 tbsp.	guava jam *	30 mL
½ cup	chopped walnuts	125 mL
1 tsp.	allspice	5 mL
2	small cantaloupes **	2

1. Mix yogurt and jam until well-blended. Add nuts and allspice. Stir well.
2. To prepare fruit, cut melon in ½ and scoop out seeds.
3. Place yogurt mixture into hollowed-out shells. Refrigerate until ready to serve.

*   *Substitute apricot or the jam of your choice.*
**   *Any melon or papaya can be used.*

Serves 4

1 Serving

Energy — Calories	237	Cholesterol	0.6 mg
— kJ	992	Carbohydrate	34 g
Protein	7 g	Sodium	56 mg
Total Fat	10 g		

Cantaloupe has been cultivated in India for over 2,000 years. It is a good source of vitamins A and C. Melons supply pure water that contains many nutrients. They refresh and aid in elimination.

Fruit Salad

Vary this delicious salad to take advantage of your favourite fresh fruit.

2	eggs, beaten	2
2 tbsp.	vinegar	30 mL
4 tbsp.	sugar	60 mL
2 tbsp.	light butter	30 mL
1 cup	Nutriwhip or whipping cream	250 mL
2 cups	seedless green grapes	500 mL
2 cups	seedless red grapes	500 mL
2 cups	drained pineapple chunks	500 mL
2 cups	drained mandarin orange sections	500 mL

1. In the top of a double boiler, over boiling water, combine eggs, vinegar and sugar, cook and stir until thick, add butter. Let cool.
2. Whip Nutriwhip or cream and fold in the cooled custard mixture.
3. Add the fruit. Refrigerate overnight.

Serves 12

Variation: *Use fresh fruit as it is available, mango, papaya, strawberries, blueberries, cherries, kiwi, peaches, nectarines, etc.*

1 Serving (using Nutriwhip)

Energy — Calories	115	Cholesterol	46 mg
— kJ	480	Carbohydrate	22 g
Protein	2 g	Sodium	39 mg
Total Fat	3 g		

Grapes have been cultivated in the Mediterranean area for over 3,000 years. There are thousands of varieties of grapes. Grapes are high in magnesium and contain some vitamin A. They aid in elimination.

Index

Index

Index

Send a *Caribbean Treat* to a friend

Caribbean Desserts, Caribbean Cuisine and ***Vegetarian Cuisine*** are $12.95 per book plus $3.50 (total order) for shipping and handling.

*Caribbean Desserts*_____ x $12.95 = $ _____

*Caribbean Cuisine*_____ x $12.95 = $ _____

Vegetarian Cuisine _____ x $12.95 = $ _____

Postage and handling _____ = $ _____3.50

Subtotal _____ = $ _____

In Canada add 7% GST OR 15% HST where applicable_____ = $ _____

Total enclosed_____ = $ _____

U.S. and international orders payable in U.S. funds./ Price is subject to change.

NAME:_____

STREET: _____

CITY: _____ PROV./STATE _____

COUNTRY _____ POSTAL CODE/ZIP _____

Please make cheque or money order payable to: **Betty K Books & Food**
3 - 1750 The Queensway
FAX: 416-283-9285 **Suite 1305**
E-mail: bettyk@idirect.com **Etobicoke, Ontario**
Canada   M9C 5H5

For fund raising or volume purchases, contact **Betty K Books & Food** for volume rates.   Please allow 2-3 weeks for delivery.

Send a *Caribbean Treat* to a friend

Caribbean Desserts, Caribbean Cuisine and ***Vegetarian Cuisine*** are $12.95 per book plus $3.50 (total order) for shipping and handling.

*Caribbean Desserts*_____ x $12.95 = $ _____

*Caribbean Cuisine*_____ x $12.95 = $ _____

Vegetarian Cuisine _____ x $12.95 = $ _____

Postage and handling _____ = $ _____3.50

Subtotal _____ = $ _____

In Canada add 7% GST OR 15% HST where applicable_____ = $ _____

Total enclosed_____ = $ _____

U.S. and international orders payable in U.S. funds./ Price is subject to change.

NAME:_____

STREET: _____

CITY: _____ PROV./STATE _____

COUNTRY _____ POSTAL CODE/ZIP _____

Please make cheque or money order payable to: **Betty K Books & Food**
3 - 1750 The Queensway
FAX: 416-283-9285 **Suite 1305**
E-mail: bettyk@idirect.com **Etobicoke, Ontario**
Canada   M9C 5H5

For fund raising or volume purchases, contact **Betty K Books & Food** for volume rates.   Please allow 2-3 weeks for delivery.

Caribbean Cuisine
by Dr. Betty "K"

Caribbean Cuisine contains traditional favourites from many islands. these recipes retain the exotic flavours of the islands and take you on an international tour of many cultures. They are also adapted to the busy lifestyle of the author and North American cooks. Fabulous appetizers and drinks, soups, salads, breads and desserts will bring island warmth and sunshine into your kitchen. The recipes in *Caribbean Cuisine* are easy to prepare and they adapt beautifully to both special occasion entertaining and family meals. Enjoy this taste of the Caribbean!

Retail $12.95   6" x 9"
120 pages   6 colored photographs
ISBN 1-919845-77-0   perfect bound

Caribbean Desserts
by Dr. Betty "K"

Caribbean hospitality is legendary. Great food and warm hospitality define Caribbean cuisine and culture. *Caribbean Cuisine* and *Vegetarian Cuisine*, Caribbean Style, by Dr. Betty "K", have gained international recognition. Acclaimed by islanders and tourists, these traditional recipes retain the essential flavours of the originals, but have been adapted to the busy lifestyle of contemporary cooks. Betty "K"s dazzling new cookbook explores the luscious variety of island desserts.

Retail $12.95   6" x 9"
120 pages   6 colored photographs
ISBN 1-894022-43-2   perfect bound